Shelby's Folly

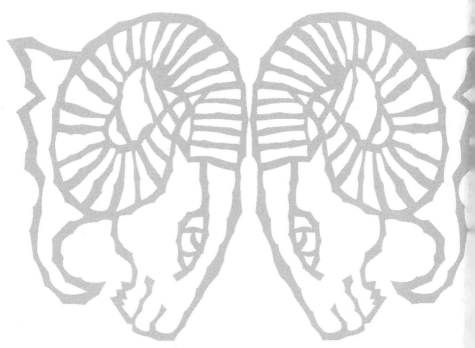

UNIVERSITY OF NEBRASKA PRESS ✦ LINCOLN AND LONDON

SHELBY'S FOLLY

FOLLY JACK DEMPSEY,
DOC KEARNS, AND THE SHAKEDOWN OF A
MONTANA BOOMTOWN JASON KELLY

All photographs courtesy
of the Marias Museum of
History and Art.

Library of Congress
Cataloging-in-Publication
Data
Kelly, Jason, 1972–
Shelby's folly:
Jack Dempsey, Doc
Kearns, and the shake-
down of a Montana
boomtown / Jason Kelly.
      p.   cm.
Includes bibliographical
references.
ISBN 978-0-8032-2655-5
(cloth: alk. paper)
1. Dempsey, Jack,
1895–1983.
2. Kearns, Jack,
1882–1963.
3. Boxing—Montana—
Shelby—History.
4. Boxing—Economic
aspects—Montana—
Shelby.
I. Title.
GV1132.D4K45 2010
796.830922—dc22
[B]
2009040609

Set in Iowan Old Style
and Madrone by
Kim Essman.
Designed by Ray Boeche.

"A curious thing about boxing is that most matches, considered intrinsically, as athletic events, are interesting only to seasoned experts and fans. The crowd at large is concerned with the issues behind them, and with the flavor of the characters involved. Each big prizefight is a climax in a story, or series of stories, about people. . . . The fight game has a way of overlapping into many of the lively social arts of man — politics, drinking, litigation, the stage, the motion pictures, popular fiction, larceny, and propaganda. That side of it, the byplay, is what appeals most to me."

John Lardner, "White Hopes and Other Tigers"

Contents

Illustrations

Following page 70

1. High Noon in Shelby

Dust kicked up around Shelby, Montana, at dawn on July 4, 1923, as thousands of people started venturing into the streets. From cots in overcrowded hotel lobbies, sleeping cars on railroad sidings, and campsites along the Marias River, boxing fans awakened to a holiday festival before the heavyweight championship fight between Jack Dempsey and Tommy Gibbons. Still more arrived by train and car, clogging the town that had hoped for many more free-spending tourists despite having no place to put them.

A livery stable had transformed itself into a makeshift lunch counter and hotel. Guests who could not secure a cot were forced to sleep on hay. Lines snaked for blocks outside proper restaurants. Souvenir vendors hawked trinkets. Green eye shades were popular items under the strong midsummer sun. Scalpers advertised their tickets, available at a fraction of face value, which was as high as $50. To one outsider reporting for the *New York Times*, the scene did not resemble a sporting capital so much as a "county seat during fair week." Bustling, but unimpressive.

All the essential services visitors lacked only emphasized the town's diminutive proportions. Oil, the source of the misplaced economic confidence that led to this heavyweight championship escapade, would not do Shelby any good today.

Local entrepreneurs did have the principle of supply and demand in their favor—at least while supplies lasted. "Food prices, which have been slowly climbing for the past several days, today cast modesty to the prairie winds and stood unashamed on the high cost of the living peak," the Associated Press reported. "Sandwiches even sold all the way from 25 to 50 cents. Steaks required large bankrolls and fresh eggs—well, there weren't any."

Thousands of tickets remained at the box office. Big crowds gathered at the gates, not to queue up for purchase, but to negotiate and agitate for lower prices. The promotion of the fight had been a financial disaster. Rather than establishing Shelby as "the Tulsa of the West," the ambition of the biggest dreamers, it cost the town a healthy percentage of its oil, ranching, and banking fortunes.

Cash-flow problems had left the fight itself in doubt for weeks. That uncertainty created a disastrous economic condition for the promoters—compound disinterest. Special trains from around the country were canceled as potential customers had second thoughts. The trains that did chug into town on July 4 ferried far fewer than the anticipated crush of fans.

"The San Francisco delegation, numbering four men, arrived early, the residue of 200, who had made reservations as soon as they heard the fight was on," the *New York Times* reported. "From Los Angeles came three instead of the expected seventy-five." That was an especially determined trio, though, considering that they came even without the fight tickets they had purchased in advance. "They were sent by mail and didn't arrive before the three customers left. So the fight fans of Los Angeles reached Shelby about the time the tickets reached Los Angeles."

Plenty of locals had tickets to spare. From Shelby to Great Falls, about two hours to the south, citizens had stepped up months earlier to make the fight a reality. They bought blocks of tickets for thousands to help raise the earnest money necessary to make the financial whales of the boxing business take notice of tiny, anonymous Shelby.

Many were stuck with thousands in souvenir cardboard, struggling to unload their inventory at going-out-of-business prices. Johnny and Tip O'Neill of Great Falls subscribed for $20,000 worth, but they could spare it. After taking one each for themselves, they returned the rest to the box office for the promoters to dispense as they pleased. Others could not afford to be so generous with their investments-turned-donations and hustled to recoup some of the cost in an overcrowded marketplace.

Unofficial box offices sprouted up on Shelby sidewalks like so many lemonade stands. In that depressed market, a ticket did not cost much more than a soft drink. Those $50 ringside seats were going for $25 or less before noon. "One Shelby citizen, who had a block of five on his hands, sold them all for $50—$275 worth of paper," the *New York Times* reported.

"Shelby citizen" was the key phrase and the reason why the rising temperature in town included both emotional and meteorological conditions. People were hot. Broken promises turned this day of celebration into an embarrassment, if not worse. Town residents had done their civic duty to crank the fight's financial engine to life, and now they were left choking on the exhaust. "Most of these well-scalped scalpers were amateur, innocent local citizens," the *New York Times* reported, "who had subscribed for blocks of tickets to help put over the great fight that was to make Shelby famous around the world."

Like the salesmen at the arena gates, they hardly could give the tickets away. Even the few people to venture into the arena early did not appear to have paid retail. An unaccompanied twelve-year-old boy from Butte was the first person through the gates at

10:30 a.m., with the stub of a ringside ticket, although he would not say where he got it or how much he paid.

Many people paid nothing, preferring to take their cars or hike up the high ridge overlooking the arena to watch from a long distance but for free. Flaherty Optic Parlor in Great Falls offered a product that could have helped their view from the hills. The "Biascope" was designed to do the work of "field glasses and binoculars of equal power at one-fifth their price." For $6, the Biascope even beat the deflated price of a ticket.

The ticket surplus created a standoff around the perimeter of the octagonal wooden arena. It was built in less than two months from pine that had to be shipped into treeless Shelby, creating suffocating construction costs that were among the burdens the promoters could not cover. That a stadium was erected at all served as a testament to their determination. But row upon row of empty seats inside, and the rowdy crowd jostling outside, symbolized the financial tug of war that defined the doomed promotion.

For most of the day, neither side budged at the box office. While that free-market duel continued, the sun beat down on the unoccupied expanse of pine boards inside, creating a surreal scene that the *Great Falls Tribune* described as "pathetic in emptiness."

There were a few thousand ticketholding fans inside, mostly clotted around the ring and scattered in the western sections of the arena. Away from the ring, and up the gradual incline of the octagon, only an occasional handful of fans could be seen, like weeds poking through sidewalk cracks.

Enough women attended to attract notice both for their mere presence and for the color of their neckerchiefs, which brightened an already shimmering afternoon. Between the tufts of bright yellow fluffed at the neck and green visors tugged low over many men's foreheads, the arena had an emerald and gold glint under the vast, unblemished blue of the Big Sky.

Brush fires of restlessness broke out as the ring remained empty long after "the alleged start of the big show," but they were contained compared to the growing conflagration outside. The early arriving crowd seemed content to amuse itself. After the announcer paged a "Mr. Leonard Diehl," a cry followed from ringside, echoing around the empty seats. "Page Mr. Raw Deal!" Touché.

Anyone without a financial interest could afford to have fun at the expense of the suckers who staged this tragicomic production. Noting the presence of famed western artist Charlie Russell, the *New York Times* could not help itself: "As a painter of the great open spaces he had the chance of his life to get distance from the vacant benches."

The sparse collection of spectators waited about ninety minutes beyond the appointed time for the festivities and preliminary bouts to begin. Even with the gates open and tickets torn, doubt lingered that a heavyweight championship fight really would happen way out there in the middle of nowhere.

A dispute over payment delayed the second preliminary bout after the first began, an hour and a half behind schedule, and ended with a second-round knockout. Mike Collins, the matchmaker, and the promoters huddled with Dempsey's calculating, manipulative manager, Jack "Doc" Kearns, behind closed doors to discuss the only issue relevant to any of the participants in this failing promotion: Money. Missing money, to be more precise.

Shelby's unpopulated white pine elephant remained far in arrears to lumber and construction contractors, to say nothing of the money owed Kearns himself, who negotiated a $300,000 guarantee on Dempsey's behalf. Despite receiving only two-thirds of that contractual promise, he succumbed to pressure at the last moment and agreed to accept the balance in gate receipts. His prospects for payment in full did not look promising. Of course, had Kearns not taken such a hard line against the promoters, casting doubt over the fight for weeks, attendance (and his take) might have been better.

Plenty of time remained for late arrivals because pockets were still being turned inside out to scrounge up the spare change needed to pay the fighters on the undercard. Kearns, of all people, ultimately put up $1,000 to keep the proceedings moving. "If this fight was in such bad condition that it touched the charitable nerve of Jack Kearns," Elmer Davis wrote in the *New York Times*, "it was pretty far gone."

Through all the frustration, the crackle of electricity still could be felt. Several airplanes flew low over the arena in violation of restricted airspace. Photographers of both the still and the moving varieties jockeyed for position at ringside and on high towers built into the stands.

When the fighters for the first preliminary bout finally appeared, fidgety fans from the rampart sections streamed past the ushers—all military veterans, in uniform—to claim empty seats at ringside. A knockout early in the second round sated some of their bloodlust, but the boxers yielded the stage to an elaborate musical interlude between fights.

Two bands—one from the Elks Club, another from the Canadian highlands, complete with kilted bagpipers—could not hold their attention. Two soloists, including a blind soldier and fight manager named J. C. McMahon, generated appreciative applause, but the people who bothered to show up were there to see a fight, not a concert.

A contingent of about one hundred members of the region's native Blackfoot tribe filed into the arena and took their seats. They wore face paint and feathers and ceremonial dress, as if playing the complementary part to the local ranchers with their boots and six-shooters.

While the visiting crowd took in the entertainment and the local color, haggling continued backstage, where Kearns eventually surrendered the grand necessary to roust the fighters for the second preliminary. There would not be a third. The repeated delays forced the elimination of that portion of the program, the better to appease a crowd growing more agitated as the clock ticked toward two hours past the promised 2:00 p.m. bell for the main event.

All the haggling and tension inside had nothing on the toe-to-toe intensity outside. Combatants in this commercial scrap included, not just sellers and potential buyers, but the IRS itself, which could be almost as persuasive as Kearns in accumulating its cut of the box office receipts. Still, Charles Rasmussen, a federal collector of internal revenue, would need at least the staff of twenty accompanying him to do that.

Kearns, in effect the proprietor of this mom-and-pop shop for the day, spent plenty of time before the fight overseeing sales, such as they were. As practical as he was cunning, Kearns did the cost-benefit analysis in his head and instructed the sellers to reduce the general admission price from $22 to $10. When that did not move enough tickets, he dropped the price again, to $8.

First cash, then gate-crashers passed through the wire fence around the arena. Between the legitimate, cut-rate transactions and the scofflaws who squirmed through for free, attendance increased by only a few hundred. To stem the flow of freeloaders, Rasmussen shut off ticket sales and ordered all the gates closed.

That left a stadium built for forty thousand with "but a few thousand souls pocketed within its huge maw when the heavy champion of the world and his challenger came down to fight."

Jack Dempsey ducked between the ropes wearing white silk trunks strung with a red, white, and blue belt and a thick, wool rollneck cardigan sweater. A retinue of handlers surrounded him, and photographers climbed into the ring, clamoring for a shot of the champ.

Dempsey looked like a star, tall, muscular, and tanned with his close-cropped, jet-black hair slicked back. The rough edges of his mining-town background were polished to a rugged, cowboy-movie quality after four years as the heavyweight champion. That aura of celebrity seduced spectators, otherwise inclined to distrust him as a draft dodger and a pirate of their personal fortunes, to give him a boisterous reception. They were in the presence of greatness and expressed respectful appreciation. If nothing else, they wanted to say thanks for coming all this way—even if they provided the train fare and then some.

Their applause soon reverted to the restless spirit that had pervaded the town for weeks. "Dynamite was in the air," Charles Samuels wrote. "As Dempsey sat down in his corner he was greeted by a shower of pop bottles. Everywhere he looked, men in the crowd seemed to be waving six-shooters at him."

There was real concern, probably unfounded but still unsettling to Dempsey and his handlers, that those men might just cock and fire their guns in his general direction. Local law enforcement officials were reported to have required people to empty their holsters before entering the arena, but order, let alone law, did not prevail at the gates.

Nerves were frayed to such a heightened sensitivity that a holiday firecracker exploding in the arena sent shock waves of fear through the crowd. "It had the effect of a six-gun outburst," Bill Corum wrote. "The reaction was sensational and, for one ghastly instant, panic threatened among the seven thousand cash customers."

Almost ten minutes passed before the challenger, Tommy Gibbons, appeared. In dark trunks and a worn robe with an elaborate, fading patterned design, he emerged to an ovation that far surpassed the decibels produced for Dempsey. Appreciation for the champion did not compare to an underdog kinship with the challenger. Citizens of Shelby, Blackfeet Indians from the surrounding territory, paying customers from out of town, everybody considered Gibbons one of them.

Much like Shelby itself, Gibbons accepted this fight on spec. Aside from training expenses, daily admission charges at his camp, and a cut of the film rights, he received no compensation. His respected and accomplished career had not attracted much notice outside boxing circles, creating a sense of him as a fortunate participant in this spectacle.

Living and training in Shelby—unlike Dempsey, who set up camp a couple of hours away in Great Falls—further established Gibbons as the favorite of the hometown fans. As the financial strain of hosting the fight threatened to drown the town, local citizens identified more and more with Gibbons. Blackfeet Indians held a ceremony in his honor a few days before the fight, anointing him "Thunder Chief." They all seemed to be in a quixotic quest against Dempsey together.

With the main event teetering on the verge of economic collapse since the signing of the contract two months earlier, the community rallied against Dempsey. It was his manager, Doc Kearns, who kept the entire enterprise in doubt with repeated demands for his full $300,000 guarantee, even as debt inundated the promoters. Frequent reports of potential cancellation, which Kearns fanned with his public posturing, served only to drive down attendance and ramp up public anger toward the champion.

Not until 2:45 a.m. on July 3 did Kearns agree to forsake his final $100,000 installment, assuming control of gate receipts to pay the bill. The *Great Falls Tribune* reported this as an act of gracious largesse, saying, without apparent sarcasm, that Kearns had made Dempsey "the best sportsman in the history of boxing." Up in Shelby, where the townspeople knew Kearns had $200,000 of their money already in the bank, they had a different opinion of Dempsey's flamboyant, pastel-clad manager, known in the newspapers as "Dapper Jack." They transferred that feeling to the champ, creating a sense of static electricity in the baking cauldron of Shelby's wooden stadium.

While Dempsey sat waiting in his corner, a member of his entourage held an umbrella over him to keep the beating sun off his back. Kearns laced the boxing gloves over Dempsey's taped hands. Two years of rust and two months of performing in the center ring of this Wild West circus made him anxious to the point of hyperactivity for the bell to ring.

Gibbons noticed the champion's dark tan from training outdoors and his twitchy impatience that rivaled the crowd's lust to start the fight. "Burned almost black by the sun, Dempsey shuffled restlessly in his corner, eyes narrowed and glittering," Gibbons said. "He could hardly hold still as Jack Kearns laced on the six-ounce fighting mitts."

Gibbons had a detailed plan to leave the ring as the new heavyweight champion of the world, a strategy that reflected his studious approach to the sport. He considered himself "the better boxer" of the two and envisioned a scenario that sounded simple enough in theory—bobbing, weaving, ducking, shuffling, parrying, and just generally keeping his distance. Forcing Dempsey to swing and miss, wearing himself out in the process. Then the challenger's footwork and fitness would win a battle of attrition with the champion. Simple enough. In theory.

In the ring now with Dempsey, the man with the calculated plan encountered doubt. From his corner, Gibbons watched as Dempsey, facing away from him, grabbed the ropes and pulled them like oars to loosen his shoulders and back. His bulging muscles flexed, and Gibbons swallowed hard, never more aware of the menace that pure, raw power presented to his clinical, detailed defense. At that imposing sight, Gibbons's mind wandered away from the ring, away from the opportunity ahead of him, to previous Dempsey thunderstorms he had watched as a spectator and the thought of another one threatening him.

The first violent storm roared through Toledo, Ohio, four years earlier. That was the day "the air turned red," as John Lardner put it, describing the squall that bloodied and buckled heavyweight champion Jess Willard. A lumbering but powerful fighter—the promoter Tex Rickard urged him, in all earnestness, not to kill Dempsey—Willard could not stand up to Dempsey's relentless assault. Never finding the support or protection he sought from the ropes, Willard went down with a thud seven times in the first round alone.

Rumors surfaced many years later that Kearns had laced Dempsey's gloves with plaster of paris, but the evidence has never supported the yarn that the manager himself first spun. All Gibbons knew in 1923 was that he had witnessed Dempsey tenderizing a titanic champion, forcibly removing the belt he still held.

Dempsey's most recent title defense came two years earlier against Georges Carpentier, the French light heavyweight. There were fleeting glimpses of what a smaller tactician could do to defend against Dempsey, and Gibbons took note from the stands, but the result was the same. Not even four rounds into the bout, after all of eleven minutes, Carpentier was splayed on the canvas for the second and final time. These were unwelcome but inevitable visions as the climactic moment of his career approached. "I'd seen what he'd done to Willard, to Carpentier, with his murderous punching," Gibbons said. "A single slip and I, too, might be groveling in the blood and resin as they had."

His disturbing reverie did not last. As mental smelling salts, he drew on the memories of his own experiences in the ring to snap out of it. Whatever temporary interference his imagination caused, in his heart Gibbons believed that he could do more than dance with Dempsey.

Gibbons did not fit the physical profile of either Willard or Carpentier. If anything, he represented a hybrid—skillful like Carpentier but bigger, quicker and more fit than Willard but powerful enough to punch his way out of trouble. And, as a student of Dempsey's tactics in particular and boxing in general, Gibbons believed that he had a mental advantage. Mixed together, it made for a potent emotional cocktail, the confidence of rigorous and meticulous preparation easing the menacing sensation of standing across from Dempsey.

Dozens of knockout victories convinced Gibbons that he could slug with the champion when necessary. Considering the man they called "the Manassa Mauler" would need only one punch, properly applied, to knock strategy clear across the Canadian border, Gibbons tried to summon the poise and patience to execute his plan. With a title shot in his sights, those previous Dempsey fights served as more than harbingers of a hard fall to the canvas burrowing into his psyche. They were scouting missions. "I'd studied Jack, analyzed his style," Gibbons said, "worked out a block or counter for everything I'd seen him do."

Again, his mind wandered. This time Gibbons traveled back seven years to a fight between his brother, Mike Gibbons, and Jack Dillon. Always tuned in to the nuances, Tommy noticed that his deft, deceptive brother didn't just make Dillon miss. He made him miss by the whisker of a five o'clock shadow, sparing himself the blow, and positioning himself to return fire in the next instant. "That fight had been a revelation to me," Tommy Gibbons said. Now all he had to do was replicate it against the most feared fighter of his time.

Pale by comparison to the bronzed champion, Gibbons felt primed for this opportunity. In physical condition that belied his thirty-two years, but with the seasoning only his extensive experience could provide, he steeled himself. His trainer, Eddie Kane, gave him the kind of idle instruction intended to dull the nerves, focus the mind, and pass the time.

"Box him, Tommy. Make him miss. Lots of time."

An oppressive sun baked the canvas and made the pine bleachers sticky with sap. From the anxious corners of the ring to the rows of restless spectators, heat radiated around the arena—in temperature and temperament. People already inside wanted their money's worth. The aggressive crowd outside wanted cut rates or open gates. Gibbons wanted his chance to show the gamblers who put the odds as much as five-to-one against him that he could win. Dempsey, like a bull bucking in a pen, looked like he just wanted to be turned loose.

Kane kept talking in the challenger's ear, narrating the scene in the opposite corner that Gibbons watched with such a keen interest.

"Watch him. He'll come out fast."

Gibbons acknowledged the advice with a nod, but it might as well have been a voice in his head talking. He knew what he had to do.

At last, the referee, Jim Dougherty, summoned the boxers to the center of the ring for instructions. "Jack's black eyes bored into mine," Gibbons said, but the champion's words were high-pitched and disarming.

"How are you, Tommy?"

"Okay, Jack."

After only a few words, Dougherty sent them back to their corners and tugged his tweed cap down on his forehead to keep the sun out of his eyes.

One final reminder from Kane as he ducked outside the ropes — "That left hook, watch it" — was the last thing Gibbons heard before the clang from ringside that jangled nerves for miles around. Shelby's civic clock struck high noon at 3:58 p.m. When the bell rang, the publicity stunt that spun out of control became a reality.

Champion and challenger moved toward each other again, this time dispensing with the pleasantries. Their determined tenacity now reflected the raucous, edgy scene all around them. Gibbons heard the whoops of his adopted Blackfeet brethren and the sound of Dempsey's feet skittering across the canvas toward him. As the fighters converged and touched gloves at the center of the ring, fans pressed toward the gates around the perimeter of the arena. Two tense standoffs months in the making were about to be settled.

2. Boom and Bust

Up on the Hi-Line in Montana, where the Great Northern Railroad chugged from horizon to horizon, Shelby evolved into a town almost by accident. Even its namesake did not think much of the potential there. Peter Shelby, an executive for the Great Northern, did not appreciate the gesture his fellow railroad manager Allan Manvel made in naming the town after him: "I don't know what Manvel was thinking when he named that mudhole, God-forsaken place after me. It will never amount to a damn."

Peter Shelby had good reason to doubt the town's prospects. The empty grassland and surrounding hills gave the area the feel of an asteroid crash site. Railroad officials, in their expansion west through the Marias Pass in 1891, "threw a boxcar from the train and called it a station." Shelby, Montana.

On the high plains, about thirty miles south of the Canadian border, Shelby attracted only a small population of cowboys at the end of the nineteenth century. Homesteaders swelled the population to about five thousand by 1913, but later in the decade a drought ravaged the region. It would become a common cycle in Montana, boom and bust, with Shelby as a high-profile participant in the enthusiastic overreaching and subsequent collapse born of both its own excesses and bad luck.

Enticements to homesteaders, unusually beneficial weather conditions for growing wheat, and the inflation of prices because of World War I had tripled Montana's population in the first two decades of the twentieth century. By the end of that second booming decade, however, the dust and the bust began to choke off the hope that had lured so many to the state. "Hot, brutal winds blew the soil the homesteaders so laboriously plowed. Ominous brown-grey clouds rolled across the vast horizon, denuding 2,000,000 acres and partially destroying millions more." Dead cattle littered the land, and the native grasses were rendered useless.

The value of farmland fell off a cliff, declining as much as 50 percent. Half the state's farmers lost their land. Twenty thousand farms went into foreclosure, and the state's bankruptcy rate became the highest in the country. Suffering from the drought and "a generation of reckless lending practices," more than half the banks in Montana failed from 1920 to 1926. More than two hundred never reopened, and this was at the height of the Roaring Twenties, years before the stock market crash that precipitated the Great Depression.

Many people fled as the conditions worsened. Beginning in 1917, and continuing well into the 1920s, the population plummeted, leaving 20 percent of the state's farms barren and vacant. An estimated sixty thousand people became drought refugees, most going west to Washington, Oregon, and California. Montana became the only state to experience a decline in population during the 1920s.

"The collapse of the Montana homestead movement marked the end of the frontier era in the Treasure State. An era of pronounced economic growth and unrivaled optimism was replaced by an unparalleled time of economic stagnation and tragic loss."

Shelby experienced the same economic plague that decimated the rest of the state. The influx of residents reverted to an exodus, making Peter Shelby's prediction about the town's dim prospects appear prescient. He could not have known that there was gold in those Sweetgrass Hills.

A geologist named Gordon Campbell discovered it in 1921, in the form of an oil field stretching north of Shelby toward Canada. As the closest town to the wildcat wells that started spurting oil, Shelby became the economic beneficiary of a new population spike, unique to its lubricated location. "The boom was on and Toole County began to feel the influx of all sorts of oil field workers, drillers, contractors, major company land men, geologists, plus the usual parasites of the oil country."

It began to seem like Montana's seasons were boom and bust, instead of winter, spring, summer, and fall. Hope and hardship became part of the landscape. Some people came and went, migrating like snowbirds to and from Florida, depending on the whims of the economic winds. Others rode out the storms and established the state's hardy identity.

"If Montana's history has been shaped by one telltale pattern, it is the cycle of boom-bust development. . . . It is the thing, more than any other, that has shaped our character and cultivated our resiliency. Without hope and hardship, we simply would not be."

By the summer of 1922, as the rest of the state's economy withered with its crops, Shelby was in full boom. An increase in population and name recognition transformed the empty prairie, miles from nowhere, into a destination for risk-taking big spenders.

North of town, in the sands beneath the rolling Sweetgrass Hills, the Sunburst Oil and Gas Company struck oil. The find did not mark the initial discovery in that territory, but the volume that surged into the Sunburst well in June 1922 after more than two weeks of drilling solidified the promise of the location buzzing for months. Within days, a parade of oil prospectors were drawn to "Montana, the Magnet" for a race to tap established and virgin terrain for the promise of riches beneath:

The high sign to "play ball" seems to have been hung out in all parts of Montana's oil areas, actual and potential, and the big play is on, with all the vigor and earnestness characteristic of the strong men who play the oil game with red-blooded courage and limitless energy.

Every hour of the day repeats its lesson that the race in the search for oil is to the swift in decision and the quick in action. The play is not for men of weak heart or flabby nerve. Such as these are thrust aside, ruthlessly, as a spring torrent throws out dead leaves and dried-up twigs.

That sort of thing pleases the real Montanans, tho. They enjoy the bustle and push to it. And they are holding their own with the other players drawn by the magnet of oil riches to the Treasure State.

It's real life to be here for the play.

James A. Johnson, a small-town man with a hearty ambition worthy of the Big Sky, was there for the play, arriving long before and staying forever after, the embodiment of the risk-taking Montana ethos. He rode the range for thirty-five years, acquiring a fortune in ranching, before banking and politics became his source of money and power. When oil spurted from those fields near Shelby, his financial interests soon included the bubbling crude in both his own portfolio and the rising profile of his town. He was also known to relish the stakes of a high-rolling bet, often risking five figures on the turn of a card. As the years passed and his fortune expanded, he could afford to lose plenty for the bracing thrill of a game of chance, either on a fight card or the more traditional variety.

In 1886–87, James A. Johnson was just an employee of Jim McDevitt's, wrangling cattle, many of which died from the brutal winter cold. Shelby did not exist yet—the railroad had not cut through the region on its way west—and the area north of the Marias River remained Native American territory.

A few years after that land "was opened for settlement" in 1888, Johnson established a ranch along the river about six miles south of Shelby. That's where James Jr., the third child and oldest son of James A. and Mary, was born on May 23, 1899. It had been a cold and rainy month in northern Montana, and James A. Johnson rode his horse into town to summon Ol' Doc Clark to the ranch when Mary went into labor. He had to wade across the Marias River, rising from weeks of torrential rain. By the time he convinced the doctor to travel to the ranch house—at the point of a .44, according to the family history—a sickly two-and-a-half-pound baby boy greeted them. "Delivered with only the help of a half-breed Indian woman," he was, in the doctor's opinion, unlikely to live. All Mary could see was "a little bitty body with tiny legs, arms and head."

To give James Jr. a chance to survive, Ol' Doc Clark said that Mary should swaddle him in the "clean dirt" outside under the sun. She followed the doctor's orders, and her "poor little body" grew stronger. He escaped physical danger but not the nickname he came to hate. Everybody knew him as "Body" Johnson, a name whose most infamous association would be with Shelby's greatest spectacle and most spectacular mess.

Early in the twentieth century, James A. Johnson moved his family a few miles north to Shelby proper to be closer to school for the children. His business interests in the town expanded exponentially, even as he continued his ranching. Johnson purchased the town general store and the former Palace Hotel and became the owner and publisher of the local newspaper, the *Shelby Promoter.* "At one time he owned most of Shelby," the *Great Falls Tribune* noted.

After becoming the town's first mayor in 1910—"a grand ball celebrated both Johnson's election and the birth of Shelby as an incorporated town"—Johnson served for sixteen years, spearheading its modernization. "He founded and built Shelby's first city improvements, water system, sewer system, sidewalks, and first electric lighting system, and laid out the townsite known as Johnson's First Addition, and later in the year 1922, Johnson's Second Addition to the Town of Shelby." For his civic work, Johnson never accepted a single dollar's pay, and, in 1912, when the population had reached a point to require the construction of a high school, he donated the lots.

The land Johnson owned became a particularly valuable commodity when the oil rush helped resuscitate Shelby after the hardship of the late 1910s and early 1920s. Though it did not increase Shelby's notoriety much beyond the oil industry and its investors, it did inflate the population and the demand for land.

Enter Mel McCutcheon. A "high pressure and very productive real estate dealer," McCutcheon and the Great Falls attorney Jim Speer came to town with commerce in mind. Speer, an old friend of the mayor's, worked with him to incorporate the "James A. Johnson and Company" real estate firm. McCutcheon and Body Johnson managed the business. For the first few months, it was brisk.

They subdivided land belonging to James A. Johnson adjacent to the town, selling and leasing the lots to the local newcomers. In the summer and fall of 1922, there were many streaming into town seeking their share of whatever the oil fields might produce.

McCutcheon and Body Johnson did not know much about the oil business that had literally burst into the local economy, but they recognized the opportunity. "No one had any idea how big the oil boom would be or how long it would last," Johnson said, but the first few heady months stirred excitement about the long-term potential. Visions of growth beyond their wildest dreams began to seem possible. "Before long we were advertising 'Shelby, the Tulsa of the West,'" Johnson said, "and believing it ourselves."

Widespread economic success inspired the establishment of a chamber of commerce, with a paid secretary on staff, and the new real estate company started feeling especially flush. The company sold, not just individual plots of land, but "whole subdivisions to other newcomers' real estate firms." Most of these sales were long-term contracts secured with a small down payment, a model that would not serve the company well when this boom went bust, but for the moment it, like the town itself, was a thriving enterprise.

Shelby had become, not just the seat of Toole County, but the barstool and bedroom community of the oil boom. New money needed to be spent, and Shelby provided all the frontier options. Saloons and a brothel—"Aunt Kate's Cathouse"—stood out along the dirt Main Street, modest in size, if not in services offered.

More wholesome entertainment could be found under the auspices of the American Legion Boxing Club, which formed in 1922 to promote fight cards in town as another diversion for the prospectors. Montana law allowed service organizations, like the American Legion, to stage bouts. Body Johnson was named chairman of the committee despite his admitted ignorance about the peculiar business of boxing.

Throughout the summer and fall of 1922, the Legion Boxing Club promoted fights it expected to be a great draw among the oil men. They were unsuccessful, which the novice promoter blamed on himself.

"I didn't know a darn thing about fight promoting and couldn't even talk the language of the sort of people one comes in contact with in promoting such affairs, and as for matchmaking, I didn't even know the meaning of the word," Johnson said. "It didn't take me long to find out my ignorance, as a few flop fights and shoddy matches taught me that help was indicated."

A former prizefighter named Lyman Sampson had moved into town from Minneapolis to open an army-navy store not long before. His ring career had not amounted to much, but Sampson learned enough about the sport in the thriving Twin Cities scene to assist its development in Shelby. Johnson sought his help to stir interest in the Legion's stagnant promotions. In exchange for his expertise, Sampson would receive a small percentage of the gate.

On January 26, 1923, their first successful promotion attracted a crowd of hundreds to the Liberty Theater. The main attraction was Dan Dorey, the Canadian welterweight champion, against a challenger named "Canadian" Carter in a ten-round title fight of sorts. Fighters from Great Falls and Shelby filled out the card with two brief preliminary bouts. Tickets went fast, with proceeds earmarked for a new American Legion clubhouse in Shelby for Toole County Post No. 52.

Hundreds of people filled the theater to see Dorey retain his crown with a quick knockout of Carter. Suddenly, the oil boom-town of Shelby had another source of income. "With the Liberty theater packed to the doors, the American Legion Boxing Commission pulled off its first boxing carnival in Shelby Thursday night," the *Great Falls Tribune* reported. "P. G. Britton and L. F. Sampson refereed the bouts, while James Johnson, Jr. acted as master of ceremonies, and arranged the details of the affair. The attendance seems to justify the securing of better talent and staging another series of bouts in the near future." They had no idea.

Real estate sales that followed the initial oil strike had slowed to a trickle by the winter of 1923, stalling Shelby's municipal momentum toward becoming "the Tulsa of the West." Body Johnson and Mel McCutcheon were sitting around their office one day, dreaming up ways to bring their once-brisk business back to life. Around lunchtime, Body propped his feet on the desk and paged through the *Great Falls Tribune*, where he came across an item from Montreal. A promoter there offered $100,000 to host Jack Dempsey's next heavyweight title defense.

Not a gambler like his father, Body Johnson still understood the value of a poker face. He suggested to McCutcheon that they see that Montreal promoter's $100,000 and raise him another $100,000 with their own offer. "If this fellow can make the headlines," Johnson said, "so should we." That's all he ever intended. To make headlines. Free publicity to revive his real estate business, nothing more, least of all an actual heavyweight championship fight.

But even publicity stunts come with complications. Among other things, they had no idea how to reach Jack Kearns, Dempsey's manager. They also had no idea whom to propose as a challenger to make the offer appear legit. Luis Angel Firpo came to mind, but, if they couldn't find Kearns in America, tracking down Firpo and his representatives in Argentina seemed even more unlikely. They were at a loss about where to begin.

Lyman Sampson happened to pass by the real estate office, and Johnson waved him over to ask his advice. In his personal recollection, Johnson did not describe Sampson's reaction to the idea. As far as a potential opponent for Dempsey, he had a quick answer: "Tommy Gibbons."

Exposing his limited knowledge of boxing again, Body Johnson assumed he meant Mike Gibbons, the only fighter he could think of with that surname. Sampson's explanation that Tommy Gibbons was Mike's younger brother and a rising heavyweight satisfied Johnson's curiosity, if not his sense that this scheme needed the whiff of truth to work.

"Well," Johnson said, "who in hell has Tommy ever licked?"

3. The Cerebral Slugger

Between the boxing Gibbons brothers of St. Paul, Tommy drifted around the fringes of the spotlight Mike occupied. A middleweight respected for his elusive, parrying style, Mike Gibbons began his professional career in 1907 when boxing was illegal in Minnesota. Anyone guilty of engaging in it faced fines, an ironic aside to the family's appreciation for the sport since Tommy Gibbons spent the last twenty-five years of his life as the law-and-order sheriff of Ramsey County. He never ratted out his older brother, not that the authorities would have acted. Mike Gibbons made his pro debut on a fight card that the local police chief hosted inside City Hall near jail cells that would not hold anyone that night on a charge of committing boxing in the first degree.

Everybody had to enter through a back door, presumably so that nobody could finger the police chief breaking the law in his own office building. For fights in barns and warehouses elsewhere around the Twin Cities, arrests were made, and fines often were levied, more than depleting any prize money earned in the ring.

Purses were minimal because illicit bouts could hardly be promoted out in the open. They were called "sneak fights." On a hot July day in 1908, Mike Gibbons fought in a barn at St. Paul Park. It was a brutal fight against Herb Catherwood, fifteen rounds of bloody, bruising combat that Gibbons later described as the toughest of his career. Their agreement called for the fighters to split 50 percent of the gate. That amounted to $90, leaving $45 for them to divide, for a payday $22.50 each. Gibbons actually lost $2.50 on the fight because he had to pay a $25 fine after his arrest for engaging in a boxing match.

In the open secret of the Twin Cities boxing underground, Mike Gibbons developed a reputation for his talent to elude punches, if not the law. They called him "the St. Paul Phantom." His increasing stature in the sport attracted offers for more lucrative purses around the country in legal venues. It became a prosperous profession for the elder Gibbons brother, who developed into one of the top contenders for the world middleweight crown.

A defensive, deceptive fighter as adept with his feet as with his fists, Mike Gibbons floated, not like a butterfly but like a buzzing fly, drifting within reach, then disappearing just when his opponent thought he had him. Harry Greb, a legendary middleweight known for his speed, became so frustrated over his futile attempts to connect against the blur that was Mike Gibbons that he lashed out at his manager afterward. "From now on," Greb said, "match me with one guy at a time."

Tommy Gibbons, two years younger, admired Mike as much as anyone and aspired to mimic him in the ring. He would fight Jack Dempsey and Gene Tunney in the prime of their careers, but Tommy called Mike the best boxer he ever faced. Mike probably agreed. Before the brothers staged an exhibition one night, Mike choreographed the performance for Tommy.

"Let's dance around for the first couple of rounds," Mike said. "Then in the third round, I'll let you knock me down."

"Sounds good, Mike," Tommy said. "When do you get to knock me down?"

"Anytime I feel like it."

After finishing high school, Tommy Gibbons spent two years at St. Thomas College in St. Paul before lacing up the gloves for a living in 1911. If not quite as polished as the Phantom, he possessed a lot of his brother's characteristics. Tommy looked like he had the potential to be an apparition in his own right someday.

His first two pro fights—"sneaks"—lasted five rounds each, ending with knockout victories over Oscar Kelly and Colored Brown. As a middleweight and light heavyweight, Tommy Gibbons also ventured east to display his burgeoning talent in the open. Knockouts continued as he barnstormed through New York, Philadelphia, Buffalo, and sometimes just over the border to Wisconsin, where the bouts were legal and very successful promotions.

Along with the Gibbons brothers, many talented and popular contenders emerged from Minnesota, a breeding ground for fighters despite the clandestine discomfort of doing business. "Sneak fights were held in gymnasiums, small halls and barns in the winter and in deeply-wooded spots along the Mississippi and St. Croix rivers in the summer."

The success of legal fights just a few miles east across the Wisconsin border eventually made the scofflaw scheduling moot. It also compelled legislators in Minnesota to lift the ban on boxing in 1915.

On July 12, 1915, Tommy Gibbons fought Billy Miske at the St. Paul Auditorium in the state's first legal boxing match in twenty-three years. Two hometown contenders and the novelty of the first openly promoted bout since the 1892 ban did not attract a full house. Only an estimated four to six thousand fans, about half the auditorium's capacity, paid the $5 admission to sweat through the oppressive heat inside the gym. They saw fast action from the fists of both boxers, trading blows and momentum. Although he took plenty of punches, quick feet protected Gibbons from absorbing the same kind of physical damage that he inflicted on Miske.

The resemblance to his older brother was uncanny. "It was the same old thing when a Gibbons boy is in the ring. Tommy jabbed and stabbed, and swung and cut his slower-moving, but willing and game opponent until Miske's face resembled a butcher's chopping block after the preparation of five pounds of hamburger."

Even when Miske had Tommy in apparent trouble, it just triggered the Gibbons family escape gene. At one point, Miske seemed to be pummeling his way to a knockout win with Gibbons pinned in the corner and the crowd roused for blood. With a right, a left, and another right, Miske missed, throwing himself off balance instead of knocking Gibbons to the canvas. "When [Miske] recovered his bearings Tommy was out of the corner and tight place, around behind him and smiling easily." Another Phantom of the ring.

Minnesota's boxing laws allowed only ten rounds and did not permit an official decision to be rendered. It had to be a knockout or a draw. Neither fighter went down that night, leaving the bout officially undecided in the record books. As far as the newspapers were concerned—and their decisions carried weight in the ring of public opinion—Gibbons won by a "wide margin."

He might have won in the ring, but Gibbons lost some money in the bargain. Fighting for 25 percent of the gross gate receipts, he earned $1,425.50—not bad for a night's work. Considering he had turned down an offer for a $2,500 flat fee to gamble on a percentage of the gate instead, he left more than $1,000 on the table.

A payday of $1,425.50 in 1915 was still well worth the effort, and Gibbons continued to make his living in the boxing business with a few more successful fights each year. He fought four times in 1916, seven in 1917, nine in 1918 and 1919, and another eight bouts in 1920. His record included several no-decisions but no defeats.

Both his reputation and his weight were increasing. Adding a few pounds and a powerful knockout punch to his deceptive repertoire allowed Gibbons to move up in class—weight—and otherwise. More than a mere competitor, he grew into a contender. In 1921 his record shows twenty-four fights, with twenty knockouts and no losses, raising his profile and his potential to earn the right to fight for Jack Dempsey's heavyweight title.

Gibbons achieved that status, in part because of a lackluster heavyweight field, but also in spite of his own resistance to self-promotion. He was a quiet family man, ambitious but not boisterous about it, married with children, and content to be at home when he was not in the gym. That did not limit his prospects among knowledgeable boxing followers, who recognized his increasing legitimacy, but he did not have the celebrity profile of Dempsey or the reverence of a war hero like the light heavyweight champ Georges Carpentier.

Even as boxing insiders began to tout Gibbons as a possible heavyweight championship contender, he still doubted that his talent could take him to such heights. Watching Dempsey fight Carpentier at Boyle's Thirty Acres in Jersey City in 1921, he began to believe. "Dempsey's hitting power was impressive, but I was certain that a boxer with speed and a good left hand that carried a little authority, could beat him," Gibbons said, essentially describing himself. "After seeing that bout, I was confident I could beat either man." From Jersey City, Gibbons took his wife and two children to their summer cottage at Lake Osakis, Minnesota, to hunt, fish, relax, and perchance to dream. His anonymity in Shelby notwithstanding, he was mentioned more and more as a potential opponent for Dempsey.

Gibbons hungered for that chance. When Eddie Kane came to him one day with news that he might be next in line for Dempsey, the modest, reticent, workmanlike gym rat lit up with bravado. "If we do, Dempsey is going to receive a surprise that he will never forget," Gibbons said.

In that moment, Mike Gibbons saw his brother's quiet self-confidence revealed. For taciturn Tommy Gibbons, that private proclamation amounted to the equivalent of a Muhammad Ali soliloquy. "Every leading sport editor in the country knows that Tom Gibbons is not given to boasting," Mike Gibbons said. "He doesn't talk much."

With the championship belt he spent his professional life pursuing now within reach, Tommy Gibbons held up his end of the conversation. That increasing quotability—and respect among the boxing literati—kept his name in the papers. Still a light heavyweight according to the scales, he also considered the possibility of a shot at Carpentier's world title in that division. In his heart, he dreamed of a date with Dempsey.

"It has been my ambition for a long time to get a championship, but I have longed for the biggest of all, the heavyweight classic," Gibbons said. "I was dubious for a time, but after trying out myself in many ways I am convinced now that I have a real chance against any man living."

Even before the Dempsey-Carpentier encounter convinced him of that, he had support from some of the sport's most prominent figures. After Bill Brennan lasted a dozen rounds with Dempsey, a boxing columnist by the name of Mike Gibbons ignored his usual prohibition against nepotism and noted that his brother could show at least as well. Like Tommy Gibbons, Brennan boxed as much with his mind and his feet as with his fists. That disoriented Dempsey enough to neutralize his power, if not enough to avoid an eventual knockout. It confirmed the template for defeating Dempsey that Mike Gibbons had described in a previous column:

28

Readers will remember I pointed out that Dempsey will continue to knock out flat-footed fighters as fast as they face him, but that the shifty fellow who can keep his head should give the champion a real fight.

At that time I did not know that Brennan would be Dempsey's next opponent. Carpentier was in my mind. But along comes Brennan—a fellow not as clever as the Frenchman—and shows what can be done.

Mike Gibbons could think of nobody better suited to finish the job Brennan began than his younger brother. More objective observers came to the same conclusion, in part because Tommy Gibbons ducked punches, not fighters, and for all his craftsmanship he did not win on points alone. He packed some power in his punches.

James J. Corbett, a legendary heavyweight in retirement, wrote a syndicated boxing column. It included a lot of lamentations about the lack of technical acumen among modern fighters. Gentleman Jim liked Gibbons and not only as a technician, although his attention to cherished fundamentals probably inspired Corbett's praise. Gibbons combined his pure approach to the sport with a daring nature in choosing opponents and a slugger's punch to dispose of them. Nobody ever knocked out so many respected opponents with such consistency as Gibbons during that overcrowded 1921 schedule. Not even in Corbett's day. Not even the modern Manassa Mauler named Jack Dempsey. "No heavyweight of any era—and that includes Dempsey himself—has accomplished anything within a mile of Gibbons knockout record. Tommy has ducked no one," Corbett wrote. "He has taken on all who came. He has gone out of his way to get fights. And all except Bartley Madden were knocked out."

Dempsey himself did not figure to be knocked out against Gibbons. But Gibbons appeared to have the defensive deftness to stay on his feet against Dempsey too. As time passed between Dempsey's title defenses, time Gibbons spent enhancing his record and reputation, sentiment for a match between them grew. A little fanning from the Gibbons camp in the form of outspoken public pronouncements also stirred the embers.

"It also may be of interest to know that Tom has been collecting every available picture of Dempsey in action," Mike Gibbons wrote in his newspaper column. "He and I have been studying Dempsey's weak points on defense. One particularly noticeable is Jack's defense for a left hook or left jab. He had better improve it."

For all his polish, Gibbons still had plenty of improving to do, too. Early in 1922, his burgeoning reputation suffered a damaging blow at the hands of the man his brother once feinted into confusion and frustration. On March 13, 1922, Harry Greb's stamina sustained him in a fifteen-round battle of attrition with Gibbons at Madison Square Garden.

It was their fourth bout, with the previous three all going the distance and ending as no-decisions. A high-society crowd of fourteen thousand attended, lured in part to help support the New York Milk Fund, the charitable beneficiary of the proceeds. The event raised more than $117,000 for the cause, and fans of all social strata soaked up the raucous boxing ambience. "Society cast aside all aloofness and joined with inhabitants of the Bowery and lower east side in cheering the efforts of the boxers."

True boxing fans, to say nothing of the gamblers who made Gibbons a two-to-one favorite, were disappointed. He managed to win only three of the fifteen rounds. Early in the fight, Greb absorbed some powerful punches that had knocked out so many others. Later, with the exception of the tenth and eleventh rounds, which he won, Gibbons could not connect with the necessary force. The boxers' capacity to dance made for an appealing ballet, and both displayed durability through the occasional furious toe-to-toe exchanges, but nobody doubted who had been the better man that night. For a change, Gibbons found himself chasing a phantom.

"Gibbons, with the agility of a big black bear, followed Greb around the ring, trying desperately to land one of the punches which have gained him his present standing in the fistic world, but for the most part he was shadow boxing. Just as he would make ready, away would waltz the Bearcat and Gibbons's blows would go amiss."

Trading furious blows, the fighters set an aggressive pace. By the final round, Greb had a lead like a runner who had lapped the field, breathing just as easily too. Described as "the Pittsburgh Windmill," Greb confounded Gibbons with techniques that left him grasping and gasping. Gibbons landed some thunderous punches but not enough. His failure to impose an eight-pound advantage stigmatized him as an easy mark for Jack Dempsey, too slow to handle his additional weight.

A win, combined with the "temporary ban of public disapproval" over Dempsey fighting the black challenger Harry Wills, would have all but assured Gibbons a title shot. Instead, his loss to a 163-pound light heavyweight not considered a legitimate contender to Dempsey left the heavyweight division without an heir apparent.

From their ringside seats, Dempsey and his manager, Jack Kearns, scouted the bout. Dempsey concurred with the judges' opinion that Greb won the fight, praising him as the aggressor throughout. He sidestepped any more detailed analysis, including an answer to the obvious question, "How long would it take you to put either one of them away?" The reigning champion just smiled.

Days later, Mike Gibbons lamented that his younger brother had sacrificed some of his famous technical mastery for the sake of more power. Tommy Gibbons "can not punch any harder than he ever could, and has been ruined as a superb boxer, temporarily at least. So says his brother, the famous Phantom Mike."

Just as his opinion counted in propping up his brother as a title contender, Mike Gibbons persuaded people of Tommy's deficiency too. A couple of routine knockouts in May over Harry Foley and Sailor Martin could not restore his luster.

"Few boxers have dropped out of sight as quickly as Tommy Gibbons, who was in line for matches with Georges Carpentier and Jack Dempsey until Harry Greb clawed his way to a decision over the man from St. Paul," the *Washington Post* reported. "Since that affair Gibbons has gone back to the bushes and he has resumed his knockout career." That quiet diligence and willingness to work his way back up would serve Gibbons well.

Two factors were working in his favor to prevent a devastating blow to his career in the wake of the loss to Greb. Perceived challengers for the heavyweight championship, like the retired retread Jess Willard or the Argentinian enigma Luis Angel Firpo, held little esteem among the public. The best of them all, Harry Wills, had the misfortune of being black. That all but disqualified him, although Kearns kept propping him up as a possibility, if only as leverage to pressure promoters. Meanwhile, Gibbons just kept fighting and winning, lurking in the shadows.

Even more important for Gibbons, Greb's reputation at the time of their fight dulled the impact of the loss. Many believed that Dempsey himself might not have survived the Greb whirlwind, despite outweighing him by a couple of dozen pounds. That weight difference kept Greb from receiving realistic consideration for that championship opportunity. It did not limit idle speculation about his potential to compete against the champion. That talk probably served to help Gibbons, who at least stayed on his feet for the duration against Greb.

"It is not at all likely that if Dempsey were to tackle Greb, the champion would emerge from the encounter with fresh laurels," according to a newspaper analysis on June 29, 1922. "Greb has an unpleasant way of making all his opponents look far worse than they really are. The tactics he uses are so peculiar that ordinary boxing methods cannot prevail against them."

Despite that description of his potential to devastate even Dempsey himself, Greb figured to earn a heavyweight title shot least of all. Described alternately as a lightweight, welterweight, middleweight, and light heavyweight, he just was not big enough. After his win over Gibbons, speculation percolated that a shot at Dempsey might be in his future, but Kearns mentioned only the glorified sparring of an eight-round, no-decision exhibition, a public slight intended to keep little Greb in his place. "We would like to see Harry make some money, even if he gets mussed up a bit in doing it," Kearns said, "to convince him that the best middleweight isn't heavy enough for the big fellow in the game."

In the crowded, if not particularly compelling, pool of contenders, Gibbons continued to tread water. He lost to the right opponent, so he did not sink. But a crack at Dempsey still required winning his way into that ring. Between his loss to Greb and his next significant fight more than six months later against Billy Miske, speculation about Gibbons ranged from the hopeful (Dempsey's natural opponent) to the doleful (sparring partner for Willard). Against Miske, he had to be at his best, or the chance for a championship belt could slip away forever.

Both Miske and Gibbons were respected boxing lifers with their reputations fluctuating before the fight on October 13, 1922, at Madison Square Garden. Unknown to the public and even to most of the boxing community, Miske was a sick man. In 1916, he had been diagnosed with Bright's disease, a kidney affliction that his doctor expected to kill him within five years, fewer if he kept fighting. He kept fighting, at least for a couple of years, until he "retired" in 1920 to sell cars. When his business lost $55,000 in five months, Miske refused to declare bankruptcy, returning to the ring to pay the bills and provide for his wife and three children.

Already he had surpassed the initial prognosis, fighting dozens of times in those five years, including three bouts against Dempsey.

His engagement with Gibbons at Madison Square Garden would be his twelfth in 1922 alone, an impressive year for Miske.

Forced to choose, expert opinion still tilted toward Gibbons, qualified support that had softened in the months since he lost to Greb. In the meantime, Miske had been pushing around his opponents. "To the home town followers of both boxers it looks like anybody's fight, with whatever edge there is going to Gibbons," the *Boxing Blade* reported. "A year ago Gibbons would have been a heavy favorite, but their records in the past twelve months have changed this sentiment. Tommy has had but few fights since losing to Greb almost a year ago, while Billy has been piling up an impressive string of victories including several quick knockouts."

Visits to training camps offered no hints to help distinguish one from the other. They each appeared to be at their best—Gibbons swift at a trim 170 pounds and Miske all slugging muscle at 188, which helped hide his illness well.

As the fight approached, a pall also hung over Gibbons, who carried his own personal burden with the same stoicism as Miske. Gibbons expected to receive news of his father's death at any moment. With that heavy on his heart and his own professional survival weighing on his mind, he drifted out to the center of the ring to meet Miske.

Gibbons was at his best, still the tenacious technician with quicker feet, stronger hands, and more versatility than most of his opponents. Miske matched him only in determination, standing up to a one-sided assault. "He battered Miske to every corner of the ring from the start of the battle, and with every punch known to pugilism."

When the bell rang for the tenth round, Gibbons went to work again with his clinical efficiency, sticking a left jab to the face, and following with a combination of hooks to the body. Miske made a futile effort to swing his way out of trouble, but his flailing punches either missed or were brushed aside. Three more combination hooks from Gibbons, as if his opponent's body was a heavy bag, knocked Miske from his moorings. "Miske sank to the floor on hands and knees, his face distorted with pain," the *Boxing Blade* reported. "He then fell back on his haunches and sat with one hand pressed against his body below the belt, evidently trying to indicate that he had been hit low." Confusion engulfed the ring.

At first, the referee, Kid McPartland, began the count to ten, an indication that he did not see a foul. A signal from the ringside judge, Artie McGovern, halted the counting. McPartland went over to confer with him. The crowd howled, and Gibbons urged Miske, now slumped on his stool, to stand up and continue, but the fight ended then and there. McPartland disqualified Gibbons and named Miske the winner by default.

Gibbons leaned over the ropes and told the writers that, if he did hit Miske low, he didn't intend it. They believed him. Their consensus was that no illegal blow occurred at all, intentional or otherwise. Still, the *New York Times* did note, without elaborating, that "the majority of the critics at the ringside . . . saw the punch and endorsed the action of Referee McPartland." Given their comments and reports, most of the fight officials and newsmen did not see it that way.

William Muldoon, the chairman of the New York Athletic Commission, ordered a hold on the pay to both fighters until he could conduct an investigation. W. H. Walker, the commission's official doctor, examined Miske and found no superficial evidence of a low blow, although the physician cautioned not to consider his preliminary physical report conclusive.

Many people in attendance appeared to have made up their minds without waiting for an investigation or a medical report. Fans thundered against the disqualification as a shocked Gibbons wandered around the ring.

"Most of the newspaper men at the ringside were a unit in agreeing that Miske quit cold. It was one of the worst cases of this kind I have seen in my twenty-five years of reporting fights," Clarence S. Gillespie wrote in the *Boxing Blade*. "Had some other referee been in there he would have counted Miske out. In a way you couldn't blame Miske for what he did because this was the only way out of it. Tom had punched Billy full of holes in every one of the nine preceding rounds, making him look foolish and bombarding him with an assortment of left jabs and right crosses."

Miske left to catcalls from a Madison Square Garden audience that felt cheated, although quitting would have been as out of character for him as a deliberate low blow from Gibbons. These were two of the most respected men in boxing.

Of course, nobody really knew the courage it took for Miske just to climb into the ring. All the angry crowd could process was that a fighter facing certain defeat won on a dubious foul that his own acting appeared to precipitate. When Gibbons finally climbed through the ropes, he walked back to his dressing room "to a cheer which shook the rafters of the Garden."

At the very least, a low blow from Gibbons must have been unintentional, given his dominance in the fight to that point. Muldoon said as much at the conclusion of his investigation. He found no grounds for suspicion to justify withholding payment any longer, but Muldoon "expressed it as his personal opinion that Miske took advantage of an incident which enabled him to win on a fluke." He remained convinced—on the basis of the view from his ringside seat—that the blow was legal.

In defeat, Gibbons received more praise in print than he otherwise would have with a victory. He became a cause as much as a mere contender, a victim of an undeserving fate, which had the effect of making him a popular choice as an opponent for Dempsey.

The bizarre circumstances might have propelled Gibbons past all the contenders as a draw at the gate, an element even more important than winning to his status in the Dempsey sweepstakes.

Gillespie interpreted the controversial defeat as a competitive and commercial success for Gibbons, better for him in both respects than the victory he deserved. "He made hundreds of new friends and they will want to see him perform often in the Garden. He made a bigger card of himself by Miske's action than if he had merely gotten the decision."

Additional coverage of the fight in the *Blade* not only inveighed against the decision; it editorialized that Gibbons had become the leading title contender again in spite of it—or perhaps because of it:

Tommy Gibbons of St. Paul, who lost on an alleged foul to Billy Miske in the tenth round of a scheduled 15-round bout at Madison Square Garden, New York City, last Friday night, demonstrated that he is in form again and ready for the best heavyweights in the country.

Tommy gave Miske a decisive beating only to lose on an alleged accidental foul. If there was a foul, it must have been accidental as it is not likely that Gibbons would land a deliberate foul when he was leading by such a big margin.

It now seems quite evident that Tommy was not quite right when he boxed Harry Greb last spring at the Garden.

Tommy is again the leading white heavyweight championship contender. A match between Jack Dempsey and Tommy Gibbons right now will draw more money than any other bout in the world—with the possible exception of a Dempsey-Wills setto.

Gibbons learned after the fight that his father had died earlier that day at age seventy-two back in St. Paul. Much of the swirl of controversy—and the ironic benefit to his career—must have been lost on him as he mourned his father. But he would be back in the ring soon enough, continuing in his workaday way to earn a title shot.

After a first-round knockout of George Ashe a month later, Gibbons went ten rounds with Miske again in Saint Paul on December 15, 1922. Both boxers weighed in heavier than their previous meeting—Miske at 196, Gibbons at 182 ½. Gibbons dominated again, although he could not knock down the resilient Miske. With the exception of a few middle rounds when Gibbons protected his swelling left eye, Miske took the brunt of the blows and often failed to connect when he had clean opportunities. Worn down but not out, he endured both the physical punishment from Gibbons and the frustration of missed chances. "Game and fighting, Miske kept on to the last bell, though apparently in some distress. Gibbons seemed quite fresh at the finish."

Sentiment in Saint Paul assumed that the winner would have the inside track to fight Dempsey. After his decisive loss to Greb in March, Gibbons spent the rest of 1922 restoring his reputation to championship caliber. He had done his part, even benefiting from a little bad luck in the first Miske fight. The public clamor in his favor had diminished since the heat of that controversy cooled, but the pool of true potential opponents was lukewarm at best. Dempsey, going on two years without a title defense, had to fight sooner or later, and none of the leading contenders had as many factors in his favor as Tommy Gibbons.

4. A Shark Takes the Bait

By New Year's Day 1923, Jack Dempsey had nursed his heavy-weight title without a defense for the eighteen months since he had defeated Georges Carpentier. His manager, Jack Kearns, indicated that the champion might fight twice in 1923 but no sooner than the Fourth of July. A swirl of speculation about possible opponents and sites filled the papers.

Before the end of January, Kearns anointed Harry Wills as Dempsey's preferred challenger. Jess Willard, the forty-one-year-old former champion whom Dempsey had bludgeoned to assume the belt almost four years earlier, would be his second choice. Luis Angel Firpo appeared in most speculative accounts as another possible contender. Tommy Gibbons might have been a popular choice of boxing purists, but his name recognition among the general public did not figure to set cash registers ringing. His bump in popularity after the Miske controversy, like a presidential candidate's rise in the polls after a national convention, did not last. Gibbons, again, was just another name in a dull conversation.

Among other concerns, Wills was black while Gibbons was colorless, a pigmentation and a personality not likely to increase gate receipts in either case. Willard would have to answer questions about being washed up, and Firpo's reputation suffered from his first lackluster showing in the United States.

"The Wills match is what the public wants most of all," Kearns said, "and Dempsey is ready to sign for any reasonable terms. I have had no bona fide offer for a match with Wills but I am going to insist that it be given first consideration."

The Madison Square Garden promoter Tex Rickard backed out of a possible Dempsey-Wills bout "because of the possible adverse effect on the championship match," presumably a reference to the challenger's race. Both the New York and the New Jersey sanctioning bodies also refused to give their blessings for Willard to fight Dempsey. In what would become a familiar boxing story, an aging former champion wanted to take another swing at the title. If Willard could prove his fitness, New York might have waived its age limit of thirty-eight, but the surrounding circumstances in the heavyweight division exasperated the state commission chairman, William Muldoon.

Muldoon extended his opposition beyond just those two potential Dempsey opponents. Over "alleged commercialistic tactics on the part of promoters, excessive demands by fighters' managers and possible detrimental effects on the ring game," he banned any heavyweight title fight from happening in the state. That caused Kearns to call off ongoing negotiations with any parties interested in a shot at Dempsey. He even rejected a $500,000 offer for a fight at the Polo Grounds from promoters who promised to ignore Muldoon's fiat. He just sounded fed up with it all.

"The champion has shown that he is willing to fight any of his challengers," Kearns said. "I have done my best to match him with them. But we've had a lot of obstacles set in the way and we're going to let the whole matter drop for a while."

After that verbal clinch appeared in the papers on February 6, Body Johnson's fateful idea swept Shelby's self-appointed "promoters" into action. Their initial whim developed into serious discussions among themselves about pursuing a heavyweight championship fight. They drafted two similar telegrams. One was addressed to Kearns, the other to Mike Collins, the Minneapolis-based editor of the *Boxing Blade*, detailing the town's intentions. Body Johnson typed them over his partner Lyman Sampson's signature, preferring to keep this stunt from rousing the curiosity of the local American Legion Boxing Club he served as chairman.

Sampson went to the Western Union office to send the telegrams and joined Johnson for lunch, neither imagining that more than a few headlines would come of it. Nothing more than free publicity for the town that would translate into traffic for the real estate office. Headlines they got.

"Shelby Offers Kearns $200,000 for Dempsey-Gibbons bout."

That headline stretched across the sports page of the *Great Falls Tribune* on February 8 over a story that sounded promising: "Many who were informed of the proposed bout asked to be permitted to assist in financing and sharing in returns of exhibition. The offer is made in good faith and the money is ready to put up."

The offers wired to the promoters said as much:

TO JACK KEARNS,
MADISON SQUARE GARDEN,
NEW YORK CITY

I have been authorized by Toole County American Legion Boxing association to offer you $200,000 as Dempsey's share for 15 round bout to be held at Shelby, Montana on July Fourth, against Tom Gibbons. If satisfactory will deposit certified check for $50,000 pending final arrangements. Wire reply.

L. A. SAMPSON, *Promoter*

MIKE E. COLLINS,
TRIBUNE ANNEX,
MINNEAPOLIS, MINN.

Have wired Kearns offer of $200,000 as Dempsey share for 15 round bout between Dempsey and Tom Gibbons to be held at Shelby, Montana, July Fourth. I have been authorized by Toole County Boxing association to make you offer of $50,000 as Gibbons' share. Will deposit certified check for $10,000 if terms satisfactory. Wire answer.

L. A. SAMPSON, *Promoter*

They wired the wrong guy. In addition to his editorial duties Collins did manage boxers in the Upper Midwest but not Gibbons, as the Shelby prospectors assumed. Eddie Kane handled his affairs. Introducing themselves to the boxing world with evidence of their ignorance, the leaders of Shelby's hasty crusade revealed their impetuous vulnerability from the opening bell. It would become a debilitating weakness.

Beyond the obvious confusion in Shelby about who was who in the boxing business, it sounded like a publicity stunt to Collins. He did not give the idea much credence but responded as a courtesy. "Dempsey-Gibbons is one of the best heavyweight matches in the world today. All you will need is plenty of cash to put it over. Best wishes." Of course, they had no money, but the scheme they had in mind required none.

Kearns, who launched Dempsey's career with the same kind of unsecured dare of a wager, should have felt a kinship with those western dreamers when he received his telegram. Something less sentimental coursed through him instead. He likewise dismissed it as a transparent publicity stunt. Extensive experience in that particular form of advertising sharpened his sense of smell when he caught a whiff of one.

Kearns communicated his impression to Collins, who had sent him a telegram out of curiosity over his reaction to the offer. "A wire came back stating that he had received a wire from the

Shelby promoters offering him $200,000," Collins said, "and that he thought it all the well-known Montana bull and an advertising stunt."

Maybe the bureaucratic headaches in New York made the Montana bull seem appealing by comparison. Maybe this man among managers recognized the leverage he could exert over cow-town amateurs. Maybe he just wanted to toy with them for a few perverse laughs. Whatever his motive, Kearns called Shelby's bluff:

L. A. SAMPSON, PROMOTER,
SHELBY, MONTANA
Am interested if you can guarantee proper protection and money deposits as well as one hundred thousand to guarantee your fulfillments on contract.
Signed,
JACK KEARNS

In Helena on business, Body Johnson heard of this response in a long-distance phone call from Mel McCutcheon. "Really you could have bowled me over with a feather," Johnson said. "I had not really expected a reply, but now that we had one and some news coverage I decided to make the most of it and drag it out as long as possible."

From now on, news coverage would not be a problem. Maintaining control over the enterprise would be. Like the Chinook winds, the notion of a heavyweight title fight blew through Montana, and citizens warmed to the idea in a hurry.

"On receipt of the news, which created a greater furore [sic] than if a dozen new wells had been brought in, citizens started scurrying around and in a few minutes the first $25,000 had been pledged and wires were on the way asking participation of other Montana cities in financing the promotion," the *Great Falls Tribune* reported. "No difficulty is anticipated either in arranging the financial details or carrying through the remainder of the program."

No legal obstacles appeared to prevent a fight from happening in Montana, but Body Johnson wanted to stay in the news, so he arranged a meeting with Governor Joe Dixon. To do that he called in the services of his father, Shelby mayor James A. Johnson, a close friend of the governor who could lend credibility to the encounter. Before he bothered Dixon, James A. Johnson wanted to hear about this Dempsey-Gibbons business for himself. He got "quite a chuckle out of it" and said, "Well, let's go up and see the Governor, and see how you make out."

Dixon had no recourse, or inclination, to stop Shelby's pursuit of the fight, but he had his doubts that they could pull it off. With the air of a dubious parent who nevertheless didn't want to stifle a child's ambition, he offered his official go-ahead with the caveat that Attorney General Wellington D. Rankin should also be consulted.

For his part, Dixon could not imagine it happening and expressed that to Johnson in no uncertain terms. "Body, just where in the hell are you going to get $200,000?" he said. "Hell, man, there isn't that much money in the whole state of Montana."

"Governor, you are not too familiar with the new oil boom that we have in northern Montana, but if you would come up there you will find out that we have a lot of fast-working oil men up in that country who will be glad to help us out to finance the fight," Body Johnson said. "All I want is your official blessing so that we may proceed with our negotiations."

"Good luck," Dixon said, "and I admire your nerve in trying."

Within days, the reported amount of money raised (or, at least, promised) accumulated like a February snowstorm.

"Shelby Has $150,000 Raised for Dempsey Title Bout."

So read the *Great Falls Tribune* on February 12, five days after the news of the offer cold-wired to Kearns. Mose Zimmerman, a real estate magnate from St. Paul who also had a significant stake in the oil field, sent a telegram pledging $100,000. "Local men have already over $50,000 raised in Shelby itself, which assures that if the fight fails to materialize it will not be Shelby's fault."

Body Johnson, meanwhile, hustled off to set up a meeting with the attorney general, nothing more at this point than another public figure to use for publicity purposes. Rankin obliged, issuing an opinion that confirmed the legality of the proposed bout. No surprise there, but the headlines it generated gave the entire enterprise another layer of authority. In the interim between Body Johnson's initial meeting with Rankin and his official approval, news of the fight continued to make the papers. Judging from dispatches originating all over Montana, ticket orders and donations assured most of the necessary money within weeks, and plans were proceeding for an arena rumored to hold as many as 108,000. Reported plans for Shelby representatives to travel east to finalize the contract even preceded the attorney general's legal interpretation. That just eliminated one last formality.

Back in the Midwest, Mike Collins became the unwitting middleman, the closest thing to a neutral observer who could make the fight a reality without his own interests interfering. His original courtesy response to Shelby's mistaken telegram only encouraged them to seize on his expertise.

"A few days following another wire came, and another and another, asking me to come out, look the town over and see what I thought about it, and they would pay my expenses," Collins said. "Also that they had oil men ready to lay all the cash money on the line to fully guarantee the show."

Shelby's "promoters" had not yet responded to Kearns because they wanted to delay a meeting with him as long as possible. That way, the story would have legs before the start of negotiations brought an inevitable end to Shelby's hope of hosting a title fight. From Helena, Body Johnson traveled to Spokane, Seattle, and Portland, granting interviews about his town's quixotic quest. "At all times I was keeping in touch with my office at Shelby through Mel McCutcheon, and everything in the way of publicity was going perfectly," Johnson said. "Some questions were being asked but nothing having any serious effect to our program."

Among the questions was, What were Body Johnson's intentions? Members of the local American Legion Boxing Club knew little about this Dempsey-Gibbons business, besides what they read in the papers, because Chairman Johnson had told them nothing. That caused some murmuring that maybe he dreamed this up to be a personal boondoggle, raking in profits from the fight at the expense of the de facto local sanctioning body he chaired. For the moment, that remained an undercurrent beneath the crashing waves of another controversy.

Rank-and-file American Legion members around Montana were against the idea. The "notorious slacker" Jack Dempsey's participation made it an event the veterans felt obliged to protest. Dempsey received a deferment from service in World War I on the grounds that his family relied on him for financial support. He contributed to the war effort through participation in bouts that raised money for military causes, and he used his celebrity to help recruit shipyard workers. When he posed for a publicity photo at a shipyard in polished patent leather shoes, however, he became a symbol of a healthy, wealthy man who cared more about his image than America.

Although he was in the process of enlisting in the navy when the war ended, that photograph and a salacious court case calcified the hostile opinion of veterans.

A grand jury indicted Dempsey and Kearns, forcing them to stand trial in 1920 on a charge of conspiracy to evade the draft. Dempsey's first wife, Maxine, described letters from him asking her to support his claim that he had to continue his boxing career to support her. Maxine said that he never provided any money, and she accused him of violence against her. It took little time for Dempsey's defense to prove that he supported not only Maxine but also his parents and siblings during the war. Evidence of considerable patriotic charity work that Dempsey had performed also mitigated the case against him. The jury needed only ten minutes to return an acquittal. That wiped his legal record clean and restored much of his esteem with the public, but many veterans could not forgive him for never serving in uniform. "Dempsey, with his fur coats, fat movie contracts, and a large bank account, had stayed at home during America's greatest fight."

Loy J. Molumby, an attorney, former World War I aviator, and commander of the Montana American Legion, declined to speak in an official capacity on behalf of the state office. He believed it to be the local post's prerogative to hold the fight. As an advocate for veterans' rights, Molumby shared the membership's pervasive distaste for Dempsey because of his failure to serve. "Notorious slacker" were his words. By contrast, however, Molumby considered any title fight a welcome opportunity to dethrone the champion, all the better if that could happen in Montana:

The sooner he is whipped the better I will like it . . . and I also feel that if he fights often enough some white man will whip him and that therefore it ought to be the desire of everybody to see him fight as often as possible. . . . [If] he is ever licked I don't know anyplace in the world I would rather see him licked than at Shelby, Montana.

However, I would like to caution the post about being very careful about any entertainment that might be provided for this bird and I think it would be the smart thing for the post to do to hold aloof from any such entertainment for him and if you must entertain somebody I believe that Gibbons, in spite of the fact that he is not champion, is more entitled to the consideration of a white man.

Yours very truly,

LOY J. MOLUMBY

The local Legion post sought Molumby's opinion about its promotion of the fight in his capacity as state commander. Molumby suggested the incorporation of the American Legion Boxing Club of Toole Post No. 52, and he became a key—and, later, infamous—figure in the negotiations. His interest grew out of the promise that proceeds from the fight would be directed toward construction of a veteran's hospital in Montana.

By February 21, two weeks after the initial wires went out, a delegation from Shelby prepared to travel east to sign both Dempsey and Gibbons. There was still some confusion. Among other details, Gibbons and his representatives had not yet responded. "The first telegrams were sent to Mike Collins at Minneapolis, under the impression that he was managing Gibbons, and this caused some delay." Kearns expressed what appeared to be genuine interest, but Collins depicted the champion's manager as somewhat more suspicious. "Says he thought news dispatches was only press stuff, and Shelby people did not answer his wire. Also says he will be glad to put Dempsey in any place I am interested. Sampson, are the people there in earnest? I must answer Kearns correctly."

As these telegrams crisscrossed the country, Collins completed unrelated negotiations for a welterweight fight in Great Falls, Montana, on St. Patrick's Day. County commissions controlled boxing in Montana, and Collins had only positive experiences with the Cascade supervisory board, which handled the business in Great Falls. It was made up of "real men" like Dan Tracy and Loy Molumby, who would be prominent figures in the Shelby promotion. Collins knew them only from staging bouts in Great Falls, but they earned his highest regard and praise in print. "The commission is composed of men who are interested in boxing as a sport, not a political plaything to be manipulated for their own private interests," which made them unusual and remarkable in Collins's experience. Any involvement of men like that had to impress him as far as Shelby's prospects, no matter how dubious he might have been about what he read in their repeated telegrams.

With a bout in Montana already arranged, Collins succumbed to Shelby's high-pressure sales pitch and promised to visit. His train arrived March 11 at 5:30 a.m., before sunrise, a coincidence of timing that worked to the town's benefit. "If it had been daylight," Collins said, "I could have looked the town over in a very few minutes and would have likely stayed on the train."

Collins estimated Shelby as a town of about 750 hearty citizens, all of whom appeared to be waiting for his train. They also had a different idea than Collins did about the nature of his visit. "According to their version of my mission, the big fight was already on and all that was necessary were some little details to close up the whole affair, and that their little cow-town in the hills would surely stage the greatest international sporting event of 1923. Then the plot thickened."

After breakfast at the Silver Grill Café with what seemed like all 750 of his new friends, Collins stepped out for a look at Shelby by the dawn's early light. Seeing nothing of note along the main (dirt) road, he knew in his heart that the fight would never happen there. It shocked him that, as he put it, he "couldn't see the town." The real shock was that he could see it, all of it, swallowed in the vast grassy expanse that dominated the landscape. Shelby consisted of a few commercial buildings, some homes, and a train depot, all visible to Collins with hardly a turn of his head. Beyond that, Montana's high plains loomed, an earthen barrier barren of civilization. If there was, in fact, a middle of nowhere, this was it. Seeing the sights, such as they were, confirmed for Collins that this whole episode was "the bunk of some kind," but he developed a grudging respect for his hosts.

"Well," he said to himself, "you fellows surely have some nerve."

They had no arena, no transportation infrastructure, no restaurants, and no hotel rooms to accommodate even a fraction of the crowd a heavyweight championship fight would attract. They had nerve but, as far as Collins could see, little else. That dearth of the basics necessary to make the bout a reality annoyed him as a businessman and a boxing enthusiast. He felt used.

Just as his frustration started to ratchet up, one of his 750 hosts hustled up to him and asked his professional opinion about who would win the fight.

"What the hell fight are you talking about?"

"Why, the Gibbons-Dempsey bout, of course. What other fight is there?"

At his breaking point, Collins went looking for Lyman Sampson to tell him in no uncertain terms to bring the fight's supposed financiers together to put up the money or shut up once and for all. By 10:00 a.m. Sampson cobbled a meeting together in the mayor's office, and Collins offered his bottom line to a committee of Shelby's interested businessmen. "To start with about $100,000 to post to show good faith in staging the bout, then enough money to build an arena and about $25,000 to promote the show."

Oil man Mose Zimmerman was not at the meeting, but, as far as the committee members were concerned, he held the purse strings to make the initial down payment Collins described. When news of the potential fight first broke, Zimmerman wired from St. Paul that he would be the primary backer. Now his fellow citizens of Shelby were calling in that promissory note. A posse went looking for him. After about an hour, Zimmerman appeared in the room.

"Well, Mose, we are all ready to do business and it will cost to start with $100,000, an arena and so forth," Lyman Sampson said. "We received your wire from St. Paul stating you would finance the show. So here we are all ready."

Zimmerman was shocked. Body Johnson could not have been more surprised when Kearns responded to his first telegram than Zimmerman was at that moment. He had made his pledge in the same spirit as Johnson's initial public offering, a sort of practical joke for civic enrichment. If Shelby wanted to make an imaginary offer for a heavyweight championship fight, Zimmerman considered it his duty as a local landowner to make a faux gesture of support.

"I hope that you did not take that wire seriously as I only figured it an advertising scheme that you fellows were putting on," Zimmerman said. "Honest, I did."

Now Collins did not feel like the sucker in the room as much as Johnson and Sampson did. Collins realized Shelby's scheme had tied even its own citizens in knots. None of them knew what to believe, so they turned to Collins for his expert opinion on this latest turn of events.

"Nothing," Collins said, in the shrugging tone of a man with nothing at stake, "just another one of them things."

Loy Molumby offered the eleventh-hour suggestion to seek subscriptions from American Legion posts around Montana to raise $100,000 in exchange for ringside seats for the members in the amount they contributed. Molumby's presence, and his proposal, in effect ceded control to the state American Legion office. Proceeds still would be directed to the construction of a hospital for Montana war veterans, and he would handle much of the legwork.

Given his favorable impression of Molumby, Collins must have felt somewhat more confident that Shelby could succeed, although the confusion in the meeting overwhelmed any inkling of competence. Amid the chaos, Collins escaped and took another look around town on his way over to the depot, departure the only thing on his mind.

The next train for Great Falls would not leave until 3:35 a.m., so Collins checked into the Sullivan Hotel, ordered a 3:00 a.m. wake-up call, and settled in for his first—and last—night in Shelby. A knock at the door around nine o'clock summoned him to another meeting of civic-minded citizens. It became his personal inside joke that no town could call a meeting together quite like Shelby.

Great orations rang through the courthouse, so crowded with Shelby's passionate citizens that Collins struggled to squeeze inside. A boisterous spirit of boosterism prevailed as Molumby outlined his plan to raise the start-up capital of $100,000 with a statewide subscription drive. C. B. Roberts, a lumberman and former state senator, spoke along with a list of other dignitaries, rousing support in an atmosphere as single-minded as a political convention. By unanimous, animated consent, Shelby approved the idea as described, not as a publicity stunt, but as the real thing, a Dempsey-Gibbons fight on the Hi-Line for the world's heavyweight championship. One speaker noted that it would be worth $10,000 in free advertising for their fair town.

The revival meeting ended with Collins goaded to the podium to give the final word. Not much of a public speaker, he nevertheless felt the spirit in the room and got to talking. He corrected the estimate on the advertising value of a heavyweight title fight. "The free publicity they would receive," Collins said, "if they had to pay for the same at the regular rates would require them to sell the State of Montana over about five times to pay for it all." This news stirred them up to the point that they might not have paid attention to his more sobering message.

Collins also told them that an event of this magnitude required a promotional apparatus at work full-time at least three months in advance. That gave them a little more than two weeks to strike a deal and start spreading the word around the country for a Dempsey-Gibbons bout on July 4. He also told the high-rolling oil- and cattlemen that they would need money, at least $25,000 liquid, before anyone would take them seriously. Four times that much would be necessary to entice Kearns just to listen.

"So if they meant business," Collins said, "speed meant everything." Within twenty minutes, the crowd produced $26,500 in cash and checks.

That bounty set off a celebration that sealed the deal in spirit, where it originated, if not in sound mind, where it might have been best left to dissolve from memory like a dream. Instead, their dreams only inflated in direct proportion to either liquor or the power of their collective imagination. Since the tyranny of time loomed over them, details of the fight had to be discussed even as they whooped it up over their first fund-raising success.

Restraint must have left town on the train Collins disembarked from before dawn. They voted on the size of the arena, deciding that a capacity of 150,000 would be about right. Collins, who triggered the sudden burst of financial support, tried to tamp down the sparks of excessive expectations before an uncontrollable fire started. He suggested two options: a 10,000-seat arena with $100 tickets or a capacity of 30,000 with tiered pricing from $20 to $50.

Men from Missoula, Montana, and Calgary, Alberta, piped up from the crowd that their cities alone would send 30,000 people, so Collins and his limited ambition lost that debate. "The boys from Shelby then got indignant," Collins said, "and assured everyone that the arena would be big enough to seat everyone in America if necessary."

Despite his dissenting view of the specifications, Collins felt himself swept up in the emotion. More than nerve motivated them. Their knowledge of the boxing business lacked savvy, but their will and ability to make this fight a reality now seemed genuine. He partied along with them until it came time to catch his train.

An impromptu parade escorted Collins to the depot. Two violins, a coronet, and a banjo provided the music. A man known as Schmittie, the proprietor of the Shelby Hotel, composed a song on the spot called "Out Where the West Begins", which he sang to the tune of "Hail, Hail, the Gang's All Here." Soon the growing crowd of excited citizens caught the fever and learned the lyrics. A chorus of hundreds serenaded Collins and even assured that his luggage would travel to Great Falls with him. He lost the claim check for his trunk, so a few of the boys tossed all three from the platform onto the train and told the baggage handler to dump them all off at Great Falls. One of them belonged to their special guest, and they wanted to make sure it would be waiting for him when he arrived.

Something in the water must have overcome him because Collins sounded like a true believer by the end of his long night, gushing like one of the oil derricks in the fields. "Shelby appears to have wonderful possibilities for staging this show," Collins told the sports editor of the *Great Falls Tribune* before leaving town:

You people out here have no idea what a drawing card such a bout will be put on in this picturesque atmosphere. There is no question but [that] the influx would be large from all directions. St. Paul and Minneapolis will empty fans Shelbywards, as will Milwaukee. Spokane and Seattle are full of fans who would jump at the chance to see a bout of this caliber so near.

You have no idea of the easterners who would take this opportunity to see country about which they have heard so much in the last few years, both concerning the natural beauties and the recent oil developments.

With those kinds of expert promises swirling around, confidence became contagious. As the harsh winter began to relent to a hopeful spring, visions of a swift expansion of Shelby's infrastructure and economy began to take hold. The local paper tried to illustrate what Shelby would become. A wide panoramic photo of the town showed an empty expanse leading north to the rolling hills that rose in the distance. It filled in the blanks with lines pointing to the "proposed location" of the arena, parking areas, a rodeo, and an auto camp. "Here is Shelby, Montana, scene of the Dempsey-Gibbons fight for the World Championship, and the fastest growing city in the United States as it looks today." In that wide-angle image, less than five months from the opening bell, it was empty.

Another photo of the business district captured the Red Onion restaurant, which the author of the optimistic caption predicted would have competition soon. "By July 1st, there will be restaurant facilities for 40,000 people."

Collins arrived at his Great Falls hotel room fresh from the Shelby parade, and a bellhop delivered the three trunks to him. Selecting his and sending the other two back to Shelby, he settled down to the legitimate business on his Montana agenda. He left Shelby buzzing and, under Loy Molumby's leadership, the canvassing of the state's American Legion posts began in earnest. That required Collins to make the Shelby fight his business too, a bigger priority than anything else he came to do. Soon after Molumby sent letters and order forms to all 127 American Legion posts and called a few of the larger ones to explain in more detail, he and Collins barnstormed the state. To Butte and Conrad and Deer Run, they brought the gospel according to Shelby, soliciting money to secure the heavyweight title fight for Montana. Quotas were established based on the size of the towns, making it not so much a sales trip as a challenge to state pride. Rotary, Kiwanis, and Commercial clubs were roped into it as well, and the reception for Collins and Molumby suggested that the business leaders would be happy to do their part. "We were met royally by all," Collins said.

Back in Great Falls, a mass meeting in the Palm Room of the Rainbow Hotel raised the city's $25,000 quota with all the hustle Shelby had shown. Enthusiasm elsewhere did not translate into proceeds. Subscriptions in other towns around the state scrounged only an additional $10,000. They were not asking for handouts. Ringside tickets were delivered in the amount provided, with a money-back guarantee. "If the match was not made," Collins said, "the money was to be returned." Beyond Shelby and Great Falls, the nearest city of substantial size, citizens did not show the same spirit as measured by payment in advance. Between the two vested towns and the rest of Montana, the fight's bank account now showed a balance of $61,500.

Dangling the carrot of hosting Dempsey's training camp prodded the game Great Falls crowd to dispense another $25,000 from their pockets. Molumby called the American Legion post in Shelby to discuss the possibility of its members subsidizing the final $25,000 to cover the earnest money necessary to entice Kearns. "They agreed to hold another of their famous meetings at the town hall that night if Molumby and myself would attend," Collins said. "All was settled and we took an auto and drove eighty miles to Shelby that afternoon. The roads were bad and it was 10 p.m. when we arrived, but faithful old Shelby was all there to a man waiting in the old town hall."

Just as Molumby and Collins completed the review of their fund-raising to date, Mayor James A. Johnson returned from an irrigation project on the West Coast. "Finding the streets bereft of citizenry, the mayor rightly diagnosed that a meeting must be in progress and arrived in time to hear Mike Collins telling a hall full of auditors that the scrap must be put over."

He knew nothing of the momentum that had overcome the idea his son conceived. A big, round walrus of a man with a graying mustache, sturdy as a barrel full of grain at over six feet and 250 pounds, Johnson commanded attention as he entered. "What in hell is this all about?" he said, interrupting the last exhortation from Collins.

Senator Roberts introduced the mayor to Collins, who caught him up on the swift developments since he left town. Johnson wanted to hear all the details. The mayor absorbed the news and put up the first $5,000 of Shelby's final share. "Permit me to say," Collins said, "that he is one of the finest and gamest men that ever lived or ever will live in Montana." It took about fifteen minutes to raise the rest.

Now that they had enough money to be considered serious contenders for the Dempsey-Gibbons fight, they needed Dempsey and Gibbons. And an arena. Otherwise, the Shelby bout was as good as on. "But neither fighter was signed up or had even been talked to regarding the terms," Collins said. "I advised Molumby, who was then the promoter and in charge of all affairs, to get busy and raise enough money to build an arena. It was decided that that was the right thing to do but through the enthusiasm and the publicity it was neglected."

Kearns played coy with the Shelby organizers. While whirlwind fund-raising continued in Montana to collect the money necessary to pay Dempsey, his slippery manager flitted here and there without a commitment or a refusal. His whereabouts remained as difficult to establish as his opinion of Shelby's proposal. After the meeting raised the final $25,000 necessary to justify intensive negotiation and promotion, Collins fired off a quick wire to Kearns in New York, asking when and where they could meet. In his reply, Kearns waved them away with word that he could not even entertain the idea for at least ten days as he mulled the details of "several other deals." Collins wrote back, verifying the legitimacy of Shelby's offer and requesting a yes or no answer within a week. Kearns did not respond.

Little did the Shelby promoters realize, but in Jack Kearns they had found the right man to make their publicity stunt a reality but the wrong man to make it a success.

5. Sticky Fingers

Jack Kearns told so many lies even he lost track of the truth. His gift for fiction did not trouble his conscience; he just considered it good business. In the decade after World War I, business was never better. By then, the erstwhile Alaskan gold prospector, immigrant smuggler, semipro pitcher, and prizefighter had wandered into an occupation perfect for his appetites and appreciation for the art of embellishment. Nobody published help-wanted ads for boxing managers. They just emerged from the primordial ooze. Kearns became the Darwinian exemplar of his chosen profession, the fittest, as if the evolutionary chart ended with a rail-thin man in a multicolored pastel ensemble and a straw boater. He put the ooze in schmooze.

His youth infused him with a sense of romance for rootless wandering in search of the next gold strike. Born John Leo McKernan in Michigan, raised in North Dakota and later in Washington

State, the boy who became Jack "Doc" Kearns followed his father on what felt like great adventures. Stories of his father's younger days stirred young Jack's imagination even more and stoked his curiosity for the view over the next hill. The elder McKernan's greatest success came in Montana, where he owned a gold mine, acquiring $100,000 and stories that became "one of the great entertainments of my boyhood," Kearns said.

As winter blew into the Montana wilderness in the late 1870s with the season's first blizzard, McKernan sensed the impending end of his gold mining fortune. His mine seemed to be "petering out." But, with $100,000 already in the bank and a warm cabin stocked with provisions, he didn't fear the future, an enduring family trait regardless of personal worth or the quality of shelter.

Through the whipping wind outside the cabin he heard a cry for help. Two men had collapsed in the snow. To McKernan's surprise, they were the president and secretary of his bank, who said they were stranded in the storm during a hunting trip. McKernan fed them, retrieved their packs from the drifts, and gave them snowshoes for the trek back into town. They had another destination in mind, although nobody ever discovered exactly where they went. Their packs contained all the money in the bank, including McKernan's $100,000. His snowshoes assisted their getaway.

"An event many years later was to provide me with satisfactory revenge on the state of Montana for this early fleecing of my father," Kearns said. "They took him for $100,000. I got it back some forty-five years later with 200 per cent compound interest."

Settling in Seattle, McKernan opened a grocery business and worked as a newspaper writer to support his family, an existence too staid to contain his son's agitated ambitions for long. With his father's wanderlust and the whiff of money to be made wafting in on the freighters returning from the Alaskan Klondike, Jack lit out for the alluring unknown territory to the north. Rather than "waste [his] young manhood on the sixth reader," he slipped out of his house one night in 1896 and stowed away aboard the *Skookum*. He was fifteen but already brazen in his pursuit of wealth and adventure.

His illicit presence on the freighter was discovered soon enough, and the captain ordered Kearns to work his way to Alaska and back. The ship anchored more than a quarter mile from the shore at Skagway. "I've lost too damned many there to the gold fever," the captain said. If that frigid distance didn't dissuade deserters from swimming for gold, the boatswain's constant supervision did. But Kearns didn't travel all that way, much of it as a "galley slave," only to turn around and let the shore of his boyhood dreams recede in the distance.

He bundled his sweater, blanket, and shoes with a rope, knotted it around his torso, and slipped from his bunk out onto the deck. "My heart almost stopped when I saw the figure of the boatswain perched on a coil of rope," Kearns said. "But it had been a hard day and he was sound asleep, with his chin on his chest." Careful not to disturb him, Kearns brushed past the boatswain, close enough for the sharp scent of chewing tobacco to singe the whiskers in his nose.

A campfire in the distance would be his destination. Kearns took a deep breath, held it, and slid down the stern anchor cable into the coldest water he ever felt. "Chunks of ice were floating in it," he said. Stifling a shout that would have given him away to the *Skookum* crew, Kearns thrashed toward the shore, cold and exhausted enough at times to doubt he would make it. When his numb knees bumped against some rocks, he hauled his frigid, haggard frame out of the water and sloshed toward the beckoning warmth of the fire. A warm welcome awaited him there too.

"They were rough, grimy and bearded characters," Kearns said, "but their hearts were a better grade of gold than the stuff they were looking for." With a dry blanket, hot stew, and stories of the gilded territory inland, they welcomed him to the Klondike.

For the fortunate among them, there was money to be made. Good fortune had not yet favored these soiled and generous souls, who must have looked like foreboding specters over the flickering fire, but they didn't scare off Kearns. "I've always been the optimistic kind," he said.

That optimism compelled Kearns to work his way inland to Nome, where he expected to find the luck that eluded so many people who followed the same hopeful path. Nome in the 1890s reeked of frontier transience—sweat and dirt from the unwashed prospectors, stale beer and whiskey from the saloons, perfume from the "fancy women" who also profited from the gold rush. "I thought it was marvelous," Kearns said.

Ah Kee, "a pudgy, kindly Chinaman with a long black queue," hired Kearns to wait tables and wash dishes in his restaurant. A U.S. government engineer named Herbert Hoover ate there, a rare kempt and couth customer. Kearns received room and board for his work among the otherwise rough, ragged, and ripe clientele but no money. When his shift ended late in the evening, he ventured out for the satisfaction of desires even stronger than the need for food or rest, stronger even than his desire for money. Scheming dreamer that he was, Kearns sought extravagance of experience more than mere wealth. More of the former existed in Nome, although he learned how to acquire the latter there too.

Those twin pursuits collided one night among the miners in the Great Northern saloon. Still new to this haze of smoke and liquor and lust, Kearns took it all in with what must have been wide-eyed enthusiasm. Wilson Mizner, occupied at the moment with a couple of women on his arms, a banjo in his hands, and a song in his heart, noticed the naive new kid. With flamboyant generosity, he donated a few dollars toward the cause of food for the skinny stranger. As much for his personality as for his philanthropy, Kearns felt such a kinship with Mizner that he became a glorified gofer for the gregarious man about Nome.

Aside from being the resident raconteur, Mizner served as the Great Northern's weigher. That is, he operated a brass scale on the bar to measure the precious metal miners used to pay for drinks and settle gambling debts. The exchange rate from gold dust to liquor and chips seemed fair enough, but Mizner took a small percentage for himself. He placed the scale on a scrap of thick carpet to absorb any gold detritus that might have spilled in the transaction, too fine to notice, but too valuable to waste. He didn't make change; he just filtered the carpet at the end of the night for his tips. "It was absolutely amazing how much gold dust that small piece of carpet could contain," Kearns said.

Kearns's relationship with Mizner provided an ideal laboratory to learn how to have sticky fingers and get away with it. When Mizner's financial interests turned to faro, he recommended Kearns to replace him at the scales. "He sold them on the theory that, because of my youth and apparent innocence, I would be above suspicion of any skullduggery when it came to weighing the dust," Kearns said. Above suspicion he was, but not above skullduggery.

In a variation on the proverb about teaching a man to fish, Mizner left Kearns with advice on making his own catch. Presenting him with a jug of molasses, Mizner told the young man to coat his hair with it before working the scales. Collect loose gold dust on your hands, he said, and run your fingers through your hair. Washing it out at night left Kearns with an appreciation for Alaska's natural resources. "In no time at all," he said, "I could well afford to buy my own jugs of syrup." Kearns didn't get rich pilfering gold dust, but he never quite got all the molasses washed off his fingers either. When he got his hands on somebody else's money, it stuck.

Learning how to get his hands on money would be the most valuable and enduring lesson of his Yukon experience. As a gold weigher, Kearns became the de facto director of the local Chamber of Commerce. He steered people in need of room, board, card games, or supplies toward his preferred entrepreneurs, who returned the favor with a grateful gratuity for the recommendation.

To diversify his holdings, Kearns used some of these "earnings" to buy a setup for a popular dice game called chuck-a-luck. Proving that he too could be fooled by an innocent appearance concealing a manipulative heart, Kearns hired "an honest looking fellow" to run the game. They made money but at a steadily declining rate until frustration compelled Kearns to divest his interest in this particular enterprise.

"I didn't know at the time that it was just about impossible for the dealer to lose at chuck-a-luck. The odds are fantastically in favor of the house," Kearns said. "I persuaded my partner to take the whole outfit."

Word soon reached Kearns that the game had become profitable again for his partner. A friend more experienced in the cons of the Klondike explained that, with a few adjustments, the operator could control the outcome to assure himself a steady, healthy return on his investment. "I had learned," Kearns said, "that you have to keep everlastingly on your toes to stay even a half step ahead of the other scufflers."

That necessary stance for professional preservation suited his peripatetic personality. Even amid the roistering grime of Nome that appealed to Kearns so much, he couldn't cool his heels when an opportunity presented itself. During his restless wanderings around town, he befriended some Indians and picked up fragments of their language—just enough, it turned out, to become the middleman entrusted to deliver their malamute dog teams to the town of Dawson, where a new strain of gold rush fever had started to spread. "Mizner and I made the trip to Dawson in style," Kearns said, "and at a handsome profit."

In Dawson, Kearns received his initiation into the boxing business, again at Mizner's urging. It seemed that Mizner had wagered a considerable sum, but his fighter didn't show. All the people who bet on the other guy claimed victory on account of forfeit. Through fearful tears, Mizner begged Kearns to replace the absent boxer. "Next thing I knew," he said, "I was being boosted into a makeshift ring in the back room of a squalid saloon. The room was jammed with half a hundred clamoring miners."

Bare-knuckled and barefoot, wearing only the bottoms of threadbare long underwear that exposed his knees through the frayed fabric, Kearns looked like his opponent might have after a long illness. "He was a solid block of a man, a powerful Dutchman from Milwaukee named Fritz," Kearns said. "He must have outweighed me by more than 50 pounds."

Fritz couldn't touch him. Retreating from the force directed at him, Kearns revealed his survival instinct along with the rough outline of his skeleton from knuckles to ribs, elbows to knobby knees. Two rounds passed without either fighter landing more than glancing blows. Early in the third, Kearns absorbed a roundhouse that sent him into the ropes, but he responded with an angry, impulsive fist to Fritz's nose that drew blood. Confident now, Kearns made the mistake of crowding his opponent until a quick combination left him woozy.

Through the ringing in his ears, he heard a voice from ringside encouraging Fritz to finish him. For reasons Kearns didn't fully understand, the referee stopped the fight and admonished the cheering fan for "coaching from the corner," a disqualifying offense. The referee raised Kearns's hand to signify him as the winner by technicality. This set off an understandable uproar, but there were enough happy bettors to offset the angry mob among them, and the fight ended, inexplicably, with Kearns as the winner.

He got his explanation later in a Dawson saloon. Peeling a few bills from his bankroll, just as he had done to welcome Kearns to Nome a few months earlier, Mizner handed the money to the referee. That was why he summoned tears to convince a novice into delivering him from a forfeit. With Mizner as his manager, no fighter could lose that night. "I had learned," Kearns said, "that in boxing even the manager must protect himself at all times."

Thus educated, Kearns found the appeal of the Klondike beginning to fade and the old wanderlust returning. With enough money to go home, experience to invest in the lucrative future of his imagination, and an advanced degree in the cunning ways of the world he wanted to inhabit, he left Alaska.

"This time I went in style, as a paying passenger," he said. "I hadn't made my fortune but, even so, I was going home with a few hundred dollars and an education at the hands of Mizner that prepared me for the years with Dempsey."

When he encountered Jack Dempsey in 1917, Kearns stumbled onto his greatest source of income, not that such a mercenary notion occurred to the novice manager at the time. He just needed another fighter if he had any hope of making it in his latest stab at a career. Boxing did not work out for the aspiring welterweight, who fought under the name "Young Kid Kearns." He lost to two champions, Honey Mellody and Mysterious Billy Smith. Thoughts of baseball with Seattle of the Pacific Coast League was a fleeting diversion from boxing. His curriculum vita from his first years back from Alaska reads like a rough draft of the eclectic, scheming life he lived: "A taxi driver in Seattle, a bouncer in a dive on the Barbary Coast, a dealer in a gambling house, a saloonkeeper, and a manufacturer of fire extinguishers." Kearns learned how to tell night from day, if not right from wrong.

Those selected line items from his resume overlook his first jobs along the Seattle waterfront—importer of immigrants and exporter of dogs. As he tended to do during his nocturnal wanderings, Kearns made the acquaintance of a man who offered $20 for the services of four men to row Chinese immigrants ashore. Kearns hired three others at a salary of $4 each, leaving $8 for him. "After all, I reasoned without the slightest quiver from my conscience, I had set up this job so I was entitled to the 'manager's' cut," he said. "Actually, they were getting off easy. I was only billing them 20 percent."

Their weekly routine involved rowing a dory about a half mile out to a waiting ship, where they hauled a few Chinese people aboard and covered them in fishnet as a precaution in case of revenue cutter inspection. Back at the wharf, in exchange for the smuggled immigrants, Kearns received the $20 and distributed it as he saw fit. After five or six nights of this, uneventful but surreal in the thick coastal fog, the human trafficking phase of his life ended with an underwater escape from the authorities.

With their cargo loaded, the group rowed toward the shore when a revenue cutter appeared through the fog, unbeknownst to the passengers on either boat until it was too late to avoid a collision. Everybody went overboard. Kearns decided not to worry about his cut of their earnings that night, fleeing the scene as fast as his kicking legs could propel him. In the chaos, two of the four freelance smugglers got away, and the captured pair never informed on them. Hoisting his head above the waves, Kearns could exhale again.

He then hooked up with E. J. Crandall as a delivery boy. A few pickups along his routes supplemented his income. Dogs capable of pulling sleds were premium commodities for people about to venture into the Alaskan gold country. Crandall offered his wagon drivers $10 for every dog, and he didn't quibble over how they got them. Kearns corralled a few but not without some scars from dogs resistant to this particular form of napping, so he didn't last long in that job either.

His innate restlessness compelled Kearns to hopscotch between professions. A long and earthy list of livelihoods also included stripping whale hides and wrangling livestock, all before he turned eighteen. "I was a very salty character and one well able to take care of myself," Kearns said. "After the ground I had been over, I had seen and started to indulge in just about everything available. This included barroom brawls, cow camp showdowns, no limit poker sessions, a drink when I felt like it and a growing fondness for a trim ankle."

A couple of drinks into his visit to a Billings, Montana, saloon in August 1900, Kearns overheard a man lamenting his need for a boxer to fill a fight card. As a veteran of one shove into the ring in Alaska, he volunteered.

"Y'ever fought?" the promoter asked.

"Me?" Kearns said. "Fought all over the Klondike."

He fished around his imagination for a name because McKernan sounded like too much of a mouthful for a real fighter. Pilfering the last name of a western boxer of some repute and appending a nickname to make it his own, he introduced himself as "Young Kid" Kearns.

With an offer of $10 — $15 for a good fight—he took on another "Kid" named Hogan, a fighter just as inexperienced but even more clumsy. In the back room of a saloon, he won the fight and earned his pay, if not the bonus. "The promoter paid me $10," Kearns said, "and I didn't argue."

As a young man rattling around the West, his athletic prowess had enough flash to earn Kearns a few bucks but not the sustainability to make a living. He could throw a punch or a pitch with velocity that made opponents want to keep their chins out of the way. Flitting from one opportunity to another, still in search of elusive gold, he never settled on a sport as anything more than his next stop on the way to wherever. After working himself into shape for a pitching tryout with Seattle of the Pacific Coast League in the spring of 1901, he skipped it to go back to boxing in Montana.

George Green, the one friend from his youth who could compete with Kearns in loquaciousness—"although I hadn't really started to reach my oratorical peak at this time," Kearns said—talked him into it. It was, in fact, exaggerated oratory from Kearns that gave Green the idea to look him up in the first place. "I had boasted to him of my prowess in Billings," Kearns said, "probably gilding the lily a bit in the process, as has always been my way." Green believed him and arranged a fight with a promoter in Butte between Kearns and Jolly Rogers, a boxer beyond his experience and ability. The promise of $100 for one night's work convinced Kearns to hop a freight train with Green the next day, bound for Butte.

They had an unscheduled stop en route, courtesy of a brakeman who hustled them off the train in Idaho Falls. This hobo layover revived for nine innings—and ended forever—Kearns's pitching career. A glum group of guys on the street in baseball uniforms needed a pitcher. Green used his precocious powers of persuasion to convince them that he had just the arm for them. Kearns auditioned and worked up enough of a lather on his fast ball to receive a $10 stake to be their starting pitcher. His opponent that afternoon happened to be Walter Johnson, who went on to major league immortality with the Washington Senators. Their pitchers' duel lasted until the seventh inning, when Johnson's team knocked Kearns around for four runs, giving the decision to the future baseball Hall of Famer. The loser took his ten bucks and caught the next train for Butte and the sport that he enriched—and that enriched him—with a different kind of pitching.

"Years later Johnson and I joked about it," Kearns said, "and I told him maybe it hadn't been such a bad idea for me to give up baseball for boxing after all."

Against Jolly Rogers in Butte, Kearns looked like he might have a future in the ring. After absorbing a left jab, he coiled his right arm into a roundhouse that knocked Rogers down with the sudden force of a gunshot. At the count of ten, twelve seconds into the first round, Kearns won his first "professional" fight and collected $75, validating his choice of boxing over baseball. His career as a fighter allowed him to snake through the West and make contacts that would pay dividends in the future. "Boxing was a catch-as-catch-can business in those freewheeling days,"

Kearns said. "You moved far, fast and often, and usually had a different 'manager' in every town."

By virtue of that powerful right hand, Kearns won a few with quick knockouts. Anybody who could stand up to his punches usually beat him, a fighter with no formal training and little appetite for the sport. That left him vulnerable as bouts wore on, too raw to rely on his instincts, too lethargic to elude an opponent with even rudimentary skills and conditioning. Either through a determination to improve or a desire to explore the Barbary Coast, Kearns went to San Francisco, ostensibly to look up Dal Hawkins, a fighter he met in Butte who offered to train him.

From the time of the gold rush in 1849 into the early twentieth century, the Barbary Coast district was Kearns's kind of place. "The only sin that wasn't condoned," he said, "was the smoking of a cigarette by a woman." It was the vice and violence capital of San Francisco, though not everyone shared the affinity Kearns felt for its offerings:

The Barbary Coast is the haunt of the low and the vile of every kind. The petty thief, the house burglar, the tramp, the whoremonger, lewd women, cutthroats, murderers, all are found here. Dance-halls and concert-saloons, where blear-eyed men and faded women drink vile liquor, smoke offensive tobacco, engage in vulgar conduct, sing obscene songs and say and do everything to heap upon themselves more degradation, are numerous. Low gambling houses, thronged with riot-loving rowdies, in all stages of intoxication, are there. Opium dens, where heathen Chinese and God-forsaken men and women are sprawled in miscellaneous confusion, disgustingly drowsy or completely overcome, are there. Licentiousness, debauchery, pollution, loathsome disease, insanity from dissipation, misery, poverty, wealth, profanity, blasphemy, and death, are there. And Hell, yawning to receive the putrid mass, is there also.

Dal Hawkins told Kearns he could find him at "Spider" Kelly's, a "little web of iniquity" rambunctious even by the Barbary Coast's rather laissez-faire standards. A five-foot-six featherweight,

Hawkins might have been, pound for pound, the most important boxing influence Kearns ever encountered. In a ring that filled a small room in the rear of a bar in San Rafael, Hawkins taught a sloppy slugger how to box. He shared the secret of his staggering left hook, thrown with the lethal swiftness of a cobra's strike, rather than the languid windup of a pitcher. With a dumbbell in his hand, Kearns labored to snap punches from his ear instead of cocking his arm behind his head. Whatever his knack for that knockout blow, Kearns showed an even better facility for filing information away for later use. Dempsey eventually learned that hook from Kearns, who used it himself with modest success but seemed even then to be more equipped for the role of prodding promoter.

The diversions of a wanderer, without much money and an inclination to spend what little he had on whiskey and women, dulled his competitive edge—at least as a participant in the arena. "I like to think," Kearns said, "that part of that may have been because I decided early that provoking and promoting contracted hostilities and holding coats for a price added up to much more fun and far easier profits."

He kept fighting for disposable income for a few more years, although he pursued other pastimes with more dedication. Training one day with a partner who shared his ravenous passions, Kearns and Jack Root ambled among the brothels of Salt Lake City in full sartorial regalia. As Kearns remembered it: "The dapper Root wore a red and white candy-striped silk shirt. A diamond stickpin fashioned in the shape of a horseshoe glittered in the cravat knotted carefully at his throat. Not a hair was out of place despite his exertion, which was mild by design. Conscious of the spotlessness of my own pink silk shirt, I wasn't drawing a deep breath either as I trotted along beside him."

Familiar faces, and not for their boxing fame, Kearns and Root basked in the cooing and come-on waves of women who called to them by name. A redhead with a bright smile, among other

1. When wildcatters struck oil north of Shelby, Montana, the economy—and the mentality—of the town changed.

2. Jobs in the oil fields attracted workers to the Shelby area and enlivened
a town situated in a vast expanse of northern Montana.

3. James A. Johnson, the mayor of Shelby and a wealthy rancher
and oil man, suffered the greatest financial losses in connection with
the fight that his son concocted as a publicity stunt
to increase the real estate business in town.

4. Attracting the heavyweight champion of the world,
Jack Dempsey, fourth from the right, and his entourage to Shelby
required a $300,000 guarantee.

5. The challenger, Tommy Gibbons, was happy to receive
only training expenses and admission collected from spectators
at his camp for the opportunity to fight for the heavyweight title.

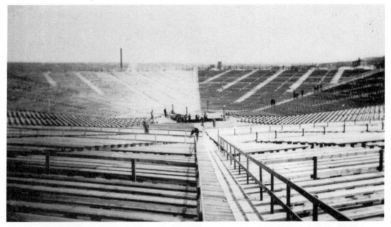

6. Contractors built a forty-thousand-seat arena in less than two months using lumber that had to be shipped into treeless Shelby. Construction costs contributed to the financial strain that threatened the fight.

7. The completed arena dominated the Shelby landscape, a testament to the commitment of the promoters and the overwhelming magnitude of the event they attracted to their remote location.

8. Tommy Gibbons, at right with coat over his arm,
received a warm welcome when he arrived in Shelby,
where he spent a month in training before the fight.

9. Jack Dempsey drew many curious spectators to his training camp
in Great Falls, where he put his power on display
against an array of sparring partners.

10. Jack Dempsey also considered himself the world champion of pinochle, a popular diversion for him in training.

11. An avid outdoorsman, Jack Dempsey enjoyed the company of a variety of critters at his training camp and spent time fishing during his stay in Montana.

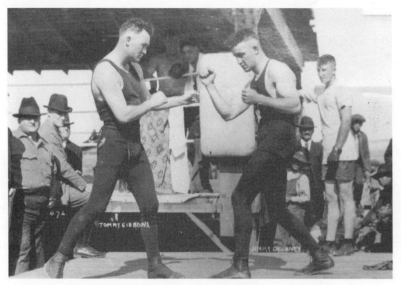

12. Tommy Gibbons and a sparring partner, Jimmy Delaney, squared off for photographers at Gibbons's training camp.

13. Tommy Gibbons's fitness for the fight was never in question, as his training regimen proved.

14. After going a few rounds with his sparring partners in front of a crowd of interested spectators, Gibbons took a break from the rigors of training.

15. Eddie Kane, the manager of the challenger, Tommy Gibbons, collected admission from spectators at the training camp, the only compensation that he and Gibbons would receive for their efforts.

16. Shelby did not attract the crowd it anticipated, but the town was bustling on July 4 and abuzz about the Dempsey-Gibbons fight.

17. The crowd was sparse inside the arena, with most people crowding around the ring regardless of the seat printed on their tickets. A few people, however, strained to see from the far reaches.

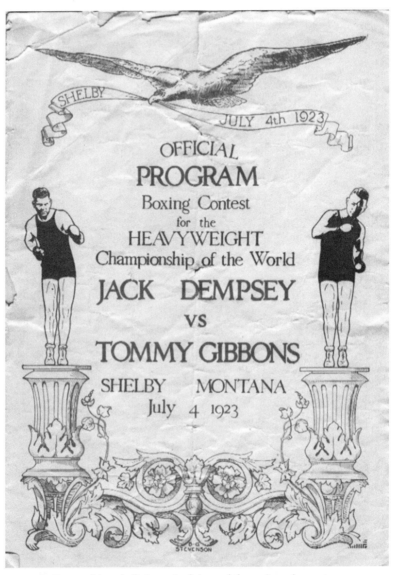

18. Fans could read all about the fight, and the curious circumstances surrounding it, in the official program.

19. As Tommy Gibbons prepared in his corner, his mind wandered to the damage Jack Dempsey had done to previous opponents and how he could avoid becoming another knockout victim.

20. When Jack Dempsey (*left*) and Tommy Gibbons met at the center of the ring for instructions, the tension in the arena—and outside the gates—reached a fever pitch.

21. Jack Dempsey's coiled power could not knock out Tommy Gibbons, a master defensive fighter who managed to stay on his feet against the champion longer than any other challenger.

22. Tommy Gibbons fought a defensive battle, and the Shelby fans threw their support behind him as he withstood Jack Dempsey's barrage for fifteen rounds.

23. After the referee, Jim Daugherty, raised Jack Dempsey's hand in triumph, a chaotic scene engulfed the arena.

eye-catching attributes, diverted Root's attention. "Now there," he said, "is something that is really something."

Jack Dempsey flitted around the edges of this world, a quieter, grimier, hungrier version of Kearns himself. Their eventual pairing would provide each with the missing piece to his professional portfolio. Dempsey had been bouncing around the West as a fighter and working in shipyards or coal mines between bouts, making a minor name for himself if not much of a living. Hardship beset Dempsey's life. Both his parents and three siblings suffered from significant illnesses, requiring his financial support whenever he did make a few dollars. Another brother was murdered in an unsolved stabbing.

While Kearns might be able to talk his way to the big time, Dempsey would have to fight for it. As Kearns recognized he had more carnival barker than boxer in him, he drifted into the role of manager, making contacts and what little money he could with his wits and a rotating roster of mediocre fighters.

It was during a visit to Salt Lake City in 1917, after his brother died, that Dempsey received a telegram from Kearns inquiring whether he needed a manager. Kearns's appreciation for Dempsey as a fighter had developed, not in the ring, but in a saloon. After a fight in San Francisco, where Dempsey dispatched the boxer Kearns managed, Joe Bond, the future heavyweight champ found himself as the referee in a barroom brawl. He rescued Kearns from certain defeat. It took a while for them to reconnect, but Kearns remembered. The telegram offering his managerial services arrived at the right time, when Dempsey had descended into unemployment and personal despair after losing his brother and then his job for returning to Salt Lake City for the funeral. Dempsey took him up on the offer, and Kearns sent him $5 and a one-way ticket to San Francisco.

"This thorny match between a fighter and his manager, the most extraordinary coupling in boxing's bristling annals, quickly bore fruit," the writer Roger Kahn said. "Kearns got Dempsey fights and Dempsey delivered knockouts. Quite suddenly William Harrison Dempsey, now and forever after called Jack, found himself confident and rising, a fighter to be noticed, a person of substance. He would never ride the rods again."

Inserting an obscure but promising fighter into a crowded picture of heavyweight contenders required Kearns to summon all his promotional panache. He lied. About money.

One day in Chicago, Kearns called the press together for an announcement he knew would make news. "I have $10,000 to bet at even money that Jack Dempsey can lick any two heavyweights alive, one after the other on the same night," he said.

Dempsey felt a little uneasy about Kearns putting a price on his head.

"You don't have $10,000," Dempsey said. "You don't even have $100."

Kearns understood his current financial condition, but the lure of publicity's lucrative force put the glint in his eye.

"Don't worry," he said. "We're getting headlines, ain't we? This is the way to get a fight quick."

Dempsey got his share of fights over the next year or so, but Kearns had a better idea. In the interest of career-accelerating hype, he decided to put Dempsey on the vaudeville circuit, figuring it would be worth at least as much publicity as "knocking over the stiffs who were left." The act involved a Kearns soliloquy introducing "the next heavyweight champion of the world" and then three rounds of Dempsey in action. Afterward, Kearns would offer $1,000 he did not have to anyone in the audience who could knock out Dempsey. To avoid any complications, he planted in the audience the trainer Max "the Goose" Kaplan, who always volunteered on cue, taking a few punches and then "an artistic swan dive that never failed to delight the customers."

The manager William A. Brady, whose show business background made him a performer perfect for boxing's canvas stage, taught Kearns the importance of wardrobe and script. Brady managed two heavyweight champions, Jim Corbett and Jim Jeffries, so his résumé brought respect. His advice validated the instincts that drove Kearns to this form of athletic acting in the first place.

"Be a showman all the time," Brady advised Kearns. "Dress the part, talk the part. Playing a fight manager's role is theater. Your fighter needs every touch of color you can give him." Kearns became the strutting peacock to Jack Dempsey's snuffling bull.

"Like a strip teaser," Kearns said, "I always figured that you couldn't get anywhere without exposure." He dressed with as much ostentatious flair as his financial ledger would allow and traveled first-class, the better to live and look the part he aspired to play.

Preening in full color required the most gaudy bauble in the boxing business—the heavyweight championship belt. Strictly speaking, it would belong to Dempsey, but Kearns would treat it as his property. Managers often used the editorial "we" when describing the work of their fighters in the ring. Kearns dispensed with that formality, referring to himself in the first person, acknowledging Dempsey's contribution almost as an aside. Kearns secured the title shot himself, after all, through a chance meeting with the famed promoter Tex Rickard.

New York Giants manager John McGraw introduced Kearns to Rickard in a Manhattan tavern. Kearns remembered him from their days in Alaska, but Rickard didn't recognize him. That didn't bother Kearns as much as Rickard's passive reaction to the name Jack Dempsey. He took that personally. Bringing up those bygone Klondike escapades interested Rickard, the only opening Kearns needed to start negotiating—nagging, really, in his best con-man fashion, as coldly persistent as a glacier and even more slippery.

For all his bargaining skill, even Kearns couldn't tilt the terms in his favor without the necessary leverage. To finagle a modest $27,500 guarantee for Dempsey, he had to ambush Rickard in front of reporters during their announcement of the fight. Where and when it would take place, Kearns and Rickard could not say when they made the deal public in New York, but the heavyweight champion, Jess Willard, would receive an unprecedented $100,000. Out of gratitude for the title shot, Rickard reported, Dempsey agreed to fight for nothing. The taciturn promoter promised to pay the challenger what he could after the gate receipts covered expenses. Kearns cut him off, feigning offense, because he had told Rickard in private that Dempsey would agree to those terms. Now, in front of the reporters, Kearns promised no such thing, making an initial demand of $50,000 for the challenger.

"You're a gambler, and I'm a gambler," Rickard said. "We are gambling one hundred thousand to get you a shot at the title. You are gambling for millions."

The gambler in Kearns gave way to the haggler in him, and he started toying with the unsuspecting Rickard. The element of surprise became his leverage. Rickard would go no higher than $25,000, so Kearns suggested leaving it up to the reporters. A dozen scribbled amounts on paper, six voting for $30,000, six for $25,000. "All right," Kearns said, "let's split the difference and make it twenty-seven five."

Considering what Willard, a six-foot-seven, 245-pound mound of gristle, feared he would do to Dempsey, an insurance policy might have been a wise investment of that share. Six years earlier, Willard threw a right uppercut that knocked John "Bull" Young unconscious and left him in such a twisted heap on the canvas that spectators thought the punch or the fall had snapped his spinal cord. It did cause hemorrhaging in his brain, and Young died the next day. Willard was arrested, although Los Angeles authorities dropped the manslaughter charge within days.

When he opened training for the fight in Toledo, Ohio, the haunted Willard asked for protection from prosecution if he killed Dempsey in the ring. Kearns roared in response, either truly offended or recognizing the promotional opportunity. Probably a little of both.

"He couldn't kill a midget if they gave him an axe," Kearns said, for publication. "Why, I'd fight the bum myself, and for nothing, but I might cripple him. It's that big tub of lard who's going to be slaughtered."

No question Kearns believed that last part. He put $10,000 on Dempsey, not just to win, but to knock out Willard in the first round, at ten-to-one odds. Such was his belief in Dempsey, and his contempt for Willard, that his wagering heart felt confident that he could earn $100,000 from the title fight himself with his insider information.

For half the first round, after some confusion and a brief delay at the opening bell that would have enormous consequences (particularly for Kearns's take-home pay), Willard and Dempsey waltzed. Instead of his usual barreling rush, Dempsey recognized and respected the champion's reach and power. Willard felt conflicting emotions—apprehension about hurting the smaller man too much and a hunger to whip this pretender to the title. Despite his size, Willard won most often by attrition. He took the title from Jack Johnson in 1915 with a twenty-five-round exhibition of stamina to match their heavyweight strength. Still, Willard's size intimidated even Dempsey—"I thought I was going to be sick to my stomach," he said—so the challenger eased his way within reach of the behemoth. A few punches and clinches, like the exposition in a novel, set a tone for the climax to come. "An awesome prelude, hypnotic and fraught with menace," the writer Roger Kahn said.

It might not have looked like it as they circled each other, the massive champion and the compact challenger, but Willard should have felt the menace in the air more than anyone. Dempsey destroyed him. Stepping out of the initial waltz with a jarring left to Willard's jaw, Dempsey "loosed the most devastating combination of punches in boxing history," Kahn said. A crushing hook punctuated the assault, knocking Willard into a sitting position, and breaking his cheekbone.

Summoning all his redoubtable will, Willard hauled himself up at length only to absorb another hook to his shattered cheek, this one jarring loose six teeth that rolled like dice on the blood-spattered canvas. Down again, with a woman in the crowd clamoring for a tooth as a souvenir, Willard used the ropes to climb back to his feet. Dempsey just waited, the rules of that era not requiring him to retire to a neutral corner, and began pummeling Willard as soon as he stood again. This went on for the rest of the first round and six knockdowns that left Willard drifting in and out of a hazy consciousness. If death would come that day, he would be the victim. On the sixth knockdown, the referee, Ollie Pecord, counted Willard out amid a deafening roar from the crowd. The roar drowned out the timekeeper's whistle, and, in the chaos of the ring after Dempsey's presumed win, officials determined the round had ended before Pecord's count reached ten. Willard had a reprieve, but two more anticlimactic rounds could not save him from the inevitable. A white towel of surrender flew from Willard's corner before the fourth round. Kearns lost his bet, but the title Dempsey won would prove to be valuable enough to make up for it.

The triumph gave Kearns the money and the profile to fulfill the self-image he carried home from Alaska so many years before. "From there on . . . he unlimbered the golden touch that he had been developing since he was fourteen, when he beat his way from Seattle to Nome and got a job weighing gold in a Klondike saloon."

As much as he became a magnet for other people's money, Kearns spent it with the same swift flamboyance. "A fast-buck man—coming or going," the writer Charles Samuels said. He developed a reputation as boxing's most colorful character, its most gregarious personality, its biggest spender, its flashiest dresser. As many as one hundred suits, tailor-made at a cost of about

$250 each, hung in his closet at one time. Mixing and matching colors that looked like sherbet flavors, he cut a striking figure in a rainbow array of clothes, often accessorized with a diamond ring. "He'd change clothes two and three times a day, from the skin out," his longtime associate Joe Benjamin said in *Esquire* magazine. "The night him and me were thrown out of Ciro's in London, after getting in a fight with some Australians who were razzing Dempsey, the Doc even had a cane. The waiters heaved the cane out after us."

More often than not, Kearns left saloons of his own volition, usually sometime after last call. Then the party moved to his suite. "Around Kearns," the middleweight Mickey Walker said, "every night was New Year's Eve." Down to the most mundane, everything he did took on a kind of exaggerated, cartoonish quality. He "even breathed with a flourish." Once Dempsey bludgeoned Willard to win the heavyweight title, Kearns had both the leverage and the cash flow to mix business and pleasure with all his ambitious, lusty abandon. He breathed deep of the elixir of life's pleasures, all the better to blow smoke with every exhalation. Life became a blur of liquor, a blue haze of expensive cigars, a blissful tangle of flesh, a blaring horn of headlines.

"Nobody ever had a better time with a title than Dempsey and Kearns," Samuels said. "Doc's spending startled even Broadway. He seemed to be in Texas Guinan's night club and the other sucker traps every night. He'd bet on anything, was always buying drinks for the house, picking up checks for guys he didn't even know. He seemed to enjoy living in a hailstorm of lawsuits, wild parties, practical jokes and newspaper headlines. He was a smiling guy with larceny in his heart who seemed to be able to go without sleep indefinitely and drink endlessly."

Kearns did not mind the reputation that preceded him; he cultivated it, embellishing his own legend beyond anything the rumor mill could exaggerate. Living hard and loving it, he became a happy symbol of boxing excess and ethical flexibility. If only people appreciated the streetwise intelligence that made it all possible. "Maybe I was fast with a buck, the booze, or the broads," Kearns said. "But I was always pretty quick with the ideas, too."

After Dempsey defended his title against Billy Miske and Bill Brennan in 1920, the heavyweight division did not have many compelling challengers left to offer. But Kearns had an idea. Sending Dempsey, the perceived slacker, against the French war hero Georges Carpentier would have explosive promotional potential. That his man would have to endure the burden of negative public opinion in that pairing did not interfere with his calculations, in every sense of the term. "To me it spelled a natural," Kearns said. "Handsome, dashing war hero and boxer against a scowling, murderous puncher libeled as a draft dodger. All of the prime ingredients were there for fat box office."

Among other complications, Kearns had to con Tex Rickard into believing his latest gimmick in order to promote a fight few others had given much consideration. Kearns told reporters that "sugar interests in Havana" had expressed interest in bidding on the fight, another fabrication of his fertile imagination. To put up a good front, he hired two Cuban waiters to pose as "sugar barons" and make a show of meeting Kearns for lunch at Rickard's usual restaurant. It worked. Rickard, not wanting to be left out of a big payday, agreed to match the Cuban "offer" of $300,000 for Dempsey and $200,000 for Carpentier. Kearns celebrated his swindle with the usual lavishness.

The writer Jack Miley described the scene this way: "Champagne corks popped, jazz music blared and beauteous blondes beamed on one and all as Jack Kearns threw a Bacchanalian revel in his suite at the old Belmont Hotel . . . to announce he had just highjacked Tex Rickard into a $300,000 guarantee to let Jack Dempsey fight the French war hero, Georges Carpentier."

Never had a fighter commanded so much money, a recurring theme in the Dempsey-Kearns collaboration. As an athlete and an attraction, Dempsey earned his fee on July 2, 1921, knocking out Carpentier in four rounds in front of more than eighty thousand people.

Gate receipts amounted to $1,789,238, making the phrase the fight came to be known by—"the Million Dollar Gate"—a rare instance of understatement in boxing. Kearns took his $300,000 happily, if a little ruefully, owing to "his failure to gamble on a percentage of the gate receipts, which would have been worth twice as much money," as John Lardner wrote. "'I can take a hint,' said Kearns, and proved, in later phases of boxing's business revolution, that he could."

He could also take credit, turning Rickard's promotion into a fantastic tale of his genius. It became, literally, the story of his life, "the Million Dollar Gate" evolving into his own embroidered legend to the point that Kearns used it as the title of his autobiography. But an excursion to the anonymous Montana town of Shelby for Dempsey's next title defense was an even better illustration of Doc's skillful hand in turning the pockets of unsuspecting promoters inside out.

"Of all his jack pots," the writer Jack O'Brien said, "the one he hit at Shelby, Montana, in 1923 was the most spectacular."

6. A $300,000 IOU

Shelby's "natural amphitheater," a wide valley surrounded by the Sweetgrass Hills, was the obvious choice as the site to build an arena. The location even had a combat past, albeit much bloodier and more deadly than any boxing match. As the brutal winter of 1885 melted into the spring of 1886, Blackfoot Indians, following the smoke from Sioux cook fires, stormed over the hills to steal their rival tribe's horses. "Then Blackfoot and Sioux war cries filled a battleground where warriors struggled to the death, and the only casualty lists were dripping scalps."

No remnants of that battle remained in 1923, except perhaps "the hovering ghost of a Sioux or Blackfeet warrior" wondering about (haunting?) this fight the local white men wanted to hold there on the Fourth of July.

The architect E. H. Keane had started surveying potential sites and sketching plans for a proposed arena as early as February. By late March, with excitement sweeping the region, the renderings of the arena had the grandest of ambitions. It would dwarf the Roman Coliseum (their respective specifications were compared in the paper) with room for at least 100,000 spectators. The design allowed for rapid expansion to accommodate many more, if necessary.

There was good reason to believe that many more might clog the narrow lanes of the little town nestled into the wide open West. Mike Collins said as much. As matchmaker and consultant to the American Legion, Collins sounded less like the skeptic he portrayed himself to be a few months later and more like the source of so much local confidence. "He describes Northern Montana as 'ideal,' 'virgin territory,' 'ripe,' and rides the crest of enthusiasm in predicting that the bout will go over for at least a $500,000 gate and perhaps closer to a cool million. It is his expressed opinion that a Dempsey-Gibbons bout would go over better in Montana than under Tex Rickard in Madison Square Garden. . . . Why, if Montana got the publicity which this will bring it in any other way, it would be necessary to sell the whole state three times."

By this time, the originators of the idea already had more publicity than they had ever imagined. They did not yet have an actual fight planned. Sequestered comfortably on a train somewhere between Chicago and Los Angeles, Kearns remained incommunicado, a minor inconvenience for Collins. "This occasioned the St. Paul editor-promoter little perturbation, however, since he is armed with a wire from Kearns saying that he is interested in having Champion Jack scrap at Shelby if the proposition looks good to Collins."

The ongoing delay suited Body Johnson's plans just fine. He still considered this runaway train nothing more than a stunt, destined to lose steam in good time, but not before he had shoveled all the free publicity he could buy into the engine. Traveling again to the Pacific Northwest in March, he found out that the patience of the local Legion members had worn thin. "Hell was popping on the home front." McCutcheon informed Johnson that, in his absence, the members had voted him out as chairman of the American Legion Boxing Club.

Other than the members' growing agitation, the faux promotion had gone according to plan for Johnson. He had managed to keep the publicity coming while holding off the inevitable nail in the coffin of negotiations that would eliminate Shelby from consideration and the public eye. The increasing curiosity and irritation about the progress at home complicated his stalling tactics. He needed to maintain his chairmanship to orchestrate the stunt, but he felt that he could not admit his true intentions to a membership now hopeful about hosting the fight. "Had I said anything to indicate that this was a publicity stunt you can readily see the effect that it would have had on our publicity," Johnson said, "so I was forced to take the position with the Legion that we were seriously and honestly trying to consummate a deal with Jack Kearns and that we expected to do so very shortly."

Johnson called that deception "the turning point of the whole deal." From that point on, there was no turning back. He retained the title of chairman, but now the boxing club had a vested and passionate interest in seeing the fight happen. Toole County Post No. 52 stood to receive $25,000 from the fight's proceeds in an arrangement made with Johnson at his reinstatement meeting. "Such a good job had been done on the publicity angle that my own people were beginning to get over-sold," Johnson said, "and now most of the people in and around Shelby wanted to see the fight held."

The idea of the fight had gathered so much momentum that Johnson could not admit the truth of his intentions. He had to let the circumstances play out as if he really intended for Shelby to host the fight, which many citizens now believed and hoped it would. "Maybe if I had used a little better judgment at this stage by giving my Legion associates more true information, they might have gone along with me as certainly the whole town of Shelby was benefiting from the publicity and, up to this point, no one had been hurt," Johnson said. "There never would have been a fight."

On the basis of the misinformation that Johnson did divulge, the boxing club retained him as chairman and imposed a two-week deadline to negotiate a deal with Kearns. That time passed with the exchange of telegrams but little else in the way of progress. The group decided to seek the counsel of the state commander, Loy Molumby, who suggested incorporating the American Legion Boxing Club of Toole County Post No. 52. Molumby became the manager of the club, and Johnson considered his work done. Everyone else, convinced by Johnson's own sleight of hand about the potential to make the fight a reality, thought this was just the beginning.

In all the hope and hoopla of trying to attract Jack Dempsey, another important detail went unattended. With the exception of the initial telegram to the wrong man, no effort had yet been made to negotiate with Gibbons. "They just took it for granted," Collins said, "that Gibbons would fight Dempsey for about $50,000." Securing the challenger became his top priority while Kearns dallied.

Collins left Shelby for Chicago on March 29 to meet with Eddie Kane, the manager of Tommy Gibbons. Arranging the contender's end of the deal added a new layer of complication. Kane lobbied for a $100,000 guarantee, in addition to 25 percent of both the gross receipts and the film rights. Those demands convinced Collins, once again, that Shelby's dream would not come true. Another wire to Kearns, outlining Shelby's final terms, brought a reply confirming that instinct once more. He would not agree to a $200,000 deal because he had better offers on the table. Stop.

Handing Kane the telegram, Collins said, "I guess Dempsey wants none of Tommy's game," and repaired to his room at the Morrison Hotel in Chicago to pack for a trip back to Minneapolis.

As he filled the trunk that had been to Shelby and back, Collins received a visitor. Kane, perhaps sensing an opportunity slipping away, wanted to know how much it would take to entice Kearns.

"Well, what is the use?" Collins said. "The show is off as far as I am concerned."

They made a night of it in Chicago until, around 3:00 a.m., Kane came up with the idea of cornering Kearns in Salt Lake City to demand his bottom-line, drop-dead, not-a-dollar-less amount.

"It's a long way to go just to hear a man say no," Collins said.

About forty-eight hours, to be exact, aboard the Overland Limited from Chicago to Salt Lake City, but Collins went along, only to hear a man say no.

Kearns produced telegrams with offers of as much as $400,000 for Dempsey to fight on the Fourth of July against his choice of top contenders.

"How much do you want for Dempsey to box Gibbons?" Collins said.

After wiggling around the pertinent question of whether he would agree to a fight with Gibbons at all, Kearns allowed that his price would be no less than $300,000. And it would be at least a week before he would commit to that in ink.

"I now fully decided that the Montana show was off," Collins said, starting to sound a little like an alcoholic swearing that this would be his absolute last drink.

He now had to report to Kane, who was not on speaking terms with Kearns for reasons neither seemed to recall. Collins shuffled between rooms of the Hotel Utah with the news.

Kane did not wince at the blow that Collins considered a knockout punch for a fight that probably should have been called off long before. Collins told him that Shelby never could come up with more than $300,000, maximum, and that he would be better off forgetting the whole thing.

"It was then that Kane made the suggestion that made the show possible," Collins said. "He suggested that Gibbons work on a percentage after Dempsey was paid."

Just like that, the plan received another bracing whiff of smelling salts from the matchmaker who seemed so intent to throw in the towel. Collins composed a wire to Molumby, insisting that he come to Salt Lake City as soon as possible, ready to make a deal. "Am flying to Salt Lake," Molumby replied. "Have all the money with me to close the match."

By that time, Kearns had made a definitive, negative statement on the matter, but Montana's plans had generated too much forward progress to be stopped. Even the firm declaration from Kearns that he did not intend to have Dempsey spend Independence Day in Shelby failed to diminish the state's enthusiasm. Within a couple of days, on Friday, April 13, Loy Molumby climbed aboard a 250-horsepower biplane to find Kearns. Undeterred by Kearns's statement dismissing Shelby as a potential site or his penchant for not staying in one place for more than a few rounds of drinks, Molumby went to Salt Lake City determined to negotiate.

"We're not coming back," he said, "until we have seen Kearns."

The pilot Earl Vance offered his plane for the search mission, perhaps the only way of keeping up with Kearns. A snowstorm over the Big Horn Mountains forced them to land in Buffalo, Wyoming, delaying a trip to Utah that Vance projected would take eight hours under ideal conditions. Collins arrived by train and caught up with Kearns, but they both declined to discuss the details of their meeting. Kearns left for Los Angeles before the Shelby crew landed, but Collins described the prospects for the fight as "exceedingly bright."

Vance and Molumby could not find the air mail field where they planned to land in Salt Lake City, finally settling into a field fifteen miles south of the city. They arrived to find a storm of another kind engulfing the fight. Complications arose back in Montana with the Executive Committee of the American Legion raising objections to Dempsey fighting in the state. Its members did not share Molumby's sentiment that a slacker had to compete to be defeated. Sanctioning his presence in Montana offended them. The state adjutant—and agitator as far as the promoters were concerned—O. C. Lamport, spoke for the Executive Committee in a telegram outlining the opposition:

This is to inform you that the American Legion department of Montana is not now and never has been a party to the negotiations to which Commander Loy J. Molumby is carrying on which if successful would bring Jack Dempsey to Montana for the purpose of staging a prize fight. We admire Tom Gibbons, and this is no reflection on him, but our attitude toward Dempsey is unchanged. We believe him a good man with his fists, but in time of national stress, a better riveter than warrior. The executive committee of the department of Montana had withheld comment striving to protect its commander, but his disregard of the committee has forced this declaration. If Dempsey never comes to Montana that is soon enough. We are unqualifiedly opposed to the promotion of any prize fight in Montana with Jack Dempsey as one of the participants.

This could not have helped matters in Shelby's mission to entice him, still precarious despite reports that made it seem assured, and now a matter of open controversy in the state. Dempsey's response to the Executive Committee's objection revealed how unrealistic a Montana fight seemed to him in the first place. "I have never even considered fighting in Montana," Dempsey said. "I have several better offers for fights elsewhere and have never given offers from Shelby or any other city in that state any serious consideration at all."

Molumby, as he made clear in his first correspondence related to the fight, shared the Legion Executive Committee's opinion of Dempsey. As state commander he felt an obligation to promote the fight as a means of raising money for a Montana hospital for

86

disabled veterans. Only the Toole County post had an official
connection to the bout as the supervising service organization
required by state law. "I have interested myself personally in the
promotion of the bout absolutely at my own expense," Molumby
said, "because I am interested in seeing such a hospital erected
in Montana."

Molumby wired Kearns and Dempsey that the American Legion
resistance broadcast over the telegraph wires did not represent
the opinion of the promoters. They were committed to hosting a
title fight in Shelby. Kearns wired back to Collins that he would
be in Chicago the next week and that, if he decided to make this
deal, he would summon the Montana promoters.

Curious about what the sheer volume of cash looked like, Collins asked to see it before Molumby flew back to Shelby. "To my
surprise," Collins said, "all Loy had was a notation of how much
there was in the Shelby and Great Falls banks for the fight."

Body Johnson said he flew with Vance and Molumby on this
mission, but the *Great Falls Tribune* made no mention of him. A
photo taken in Salt Lake City and published in the paper showed
Vance and Molumby alongside Mike Collins and Eddie Kane.
In any case, Johnson began to notice the potential reality of the
fight leaking through the cracks in his publicity stunt. He could
not hold back the inevitable flood any longer. "By this time I
could see that the whole program might be carried through and
it was going to be up to us all to try and see that it was," Johnson
said, "and from this time on our original tactics of publicity only,
changed to a program of honestly trying to put on the fight in
earnest."

For two months most of the parties involved, not privy to
Johnson's original intent, had been working very much in earnest
to make it happen. Because Kearns kept the hustling promoters
at arm's length, perhaps Johnson had good reason to believe the
deal would fall through eventually, the harmless endgame he
envisioned all along. His awareness of the unstoppable head of

steam the idea had generated came too late. Events had over-
taken his vision.

Molumby climbed back into Earl Vance's plane at 5:00 a.m. on
April 25 for what he believed would be the last leg of the journey
to bring a heavyweight title fight to Shelby. Collins had wired
word that Kearns was en route to Chicago and that he would sign
the contract if the promoters had the initial guarantee in hand.
Believed to be carrying a certified check for $110,000—the first
installment, plus $10,000 for training expenses—Molumby flew
with Vance to Minneapolis to pick up Collins and then to Chicago for the final formalities. Eddie Kane echoed the increasing
confidence in the fight deal the next day. He made the first public
mention of a $300,000 payday for Dempsey in the process, the
amount that would haunt the fight forever.

"There is no doubt in my mind that the only hitch of the match
is the little formality of signing the articles," Kane said. "Dempsey
has been guaranteed $300,000. I have already accepted terms
on behalf of Gibbons."

Kearns was not quite so agreeable. The undisputed haggling
champion spent three hours on April 27 discussing terms of the
deal at the Morrison Hotel with Molumby and Collins. He still
wanted the weekend to think it over, leaving town intent on
playing hard to get.

"I'll let you know Monday," Kearns said with a shrug as he
hailed a taxi for the ride to Union Station to catch an eastbound
train. Tex Rickard awaited back in New York, perhaps with a
counteroffer, perhaps as a prop in a Kearns bluff, but the deal
would be delayed at least for the weekend.

"Molumby and Collins, fighting an offensive battle with
$300,000 in cold cash, were chagrined at the flight of Kearns,"
the *Great Falls Tribune* reported in its April 28 editions, "but are
hoping that the shrewd manager will return and surrender under
bombardment."

That bombardment—and Rickard's refusal to make a comparable counteroffer—weakened Kearns's defenses. By Monday, a long-distance telephone call between Molumby and Kearns sealed the Shelby deal in principle. Kearns did not confirm Molumby's announcement of the agreement, but he outlined the details for a reporter in New York. "Molumby proposed, said Kearns, that Dempsey be guaranteed $300,000 for the fight," the *Great Falls Tribune* reported on May 1. "A certified check for $100,000 would be paid when the contract was signed, $100,000 more would be paid within a month, and the third $100,000 at least 48 hours before Dempsey entered the ring. The champion also would have the option of 60 percent of the gate receipts."

For a fight between Dempsey and Gibbons, Rickard would agree only to a percentage-based contract for the champion, even in the New York metropolitan area. "The promoter expressed doubt on the question of interest which would attract to such a bout in this district," the *New York Times* reported. Shelby's novice promoters showed no such resistance to the idea of attracting interest and paying customers to their remote location.

Dollar figures and other contractual details varied slightly in different dispatches about the negotiations, but the infamous $300,000 total appeared repeatedly in the *Great Falls Tribune* and elsewhere for at least a week leading up to the official signing. Body Johnson, sick in the hospital at the time, expressed shock and confusion at how Molumby arrived at that amount. Not only had Shelby's publicity stunt become a daunting reality; it had taken on a degree of difficulty half again as large as the original, imaginary offer.

But, in fact, it could not have come as such a shock back in Shelby. Maybe Kearns invented the amount for reporters—it would not have been the first time—but the number showed up all over the place, including that quote from Eddie Kane, the manager of the challenger. Nobody paying attention to reports on the negotiations could have been blindsided by it. "The terms were all up to Molumby," Collins said, "who after some deliberation accepted them."

What Collins described as "some deliberation" the scrambling Shelby civic leaders later translated to mean "a lot of liquor." Based on a confidence the manager of the Morrison Hotel divulged, Body Johnson said he came to believe that Kearns plied Molumby with alcohol as a final negotiating ploy to up the ante for Dempsey. "Loy Molumby was ignorant enough to go back there and let Kearns talk him in—with the help of an awful lot of Champagne and whiskey, he drunkenly signed a contract that he brought back to us that was impossible," Johnson said. "But what could we do about it? The $100,000 was in Kearns's hands now, so what could we do? We finally decided that we would try to make it work."

Molumby insisted that Kearns simply would not settle for less. The amount appeared so often in the newspapers before the signing that the legend of liquor-fueled persuasion seems apocryphal. Robert Edgren reported on May 3: "The Shelby people want to put Shelby on the map and they are willing to pay for it. They are so willing that they will put up $300,000 for Dempsey's end—the same amount Tex Rickard paid Dempsey for the match with Carpentier at Jersey City." Almost two days still remained until the final signing of the articles, so the figure that shocked Body Johnson should not have.

Johnson maintained many years later that he assumed the amount to be a misprint in the report of the official signing in Chicago. "At no time, during the period of May 1 to May 4, or before, had there ever been any mention or discussion of any cash terms other than those of the original agreement with Kearns . . . i.e., $100,000 cash and the balance of $100,000 to paid him before entering the ring on July 4."

When a nurse brought him the *Great Falls Tribune* of May 5 blaring the news of the signed contract, he was "elated." The amount must have been a mistake. Johnson said that he dismissed it in the euphoric moment, confident that the actual legal document would straighten out the misunderstanding. It remains uncertain why, if his reported reaction is accurate, he and other local promoters did not start asking questions when that number turned up in the same paper days in advance. All those references could not have been ignored as misprints or mere speculation, especially the quote from Eddie Kane, who had a seat at the negotiating table.

References to the 1921 title fight in Jersey City were significant too. Also known as "the Million Dollar Gate," that fight established, not just the appearance fee a modern heavyweight champion commanded, but the potential return on investment for promoters. As recently as four years earlier, two years before Dempsey's $300,000 payday at Boyle's Thirty Acres, Willard received $100,000 for defending his title. At that rate of inflation—a 200 percent increase for the champion in the two years between Dempsey's fights with Willard and Carpentier—Shelby got a bargain.

First, the check had to clear. All the chasing and haggling that produced the grudging agreement almost fell through a moment before the signing on account of insufficient funds. "When it came to signing the articles, it was discovered that Loy did not have the $100,000. He had a letter from Shirley Ford, president of a Great Falls bank stating that he would wire the money to the Commercial Trust and Savings Bank at Chicago," Collins said. "On arriving at the bank, we found that Ford instead of sending $100,000 had only sent $75,000. Just how he figured we were going to pay a $100,000 cash account with $75,000 was more than we could fathom."

This set off days of long-distance deliberation between Molumby and the Montana backers, first trying to release the balance of the money, and then trying to untie the strings from it. "The condition of releasing the money reminded me of an accident insurance policy I once accidentally carried," Collins said. "In order to collect any accident damages, a fellow would have to stand on a certain corner, get hit by an auto truck of a certain make with a driver of a certain nationality and personally report the damages not later than five minutes after the accident. As I did not care about getting hurt that way, I never collected on that policy, and as Ford's strings on the Montana money resembled the said insurance policy, Molumby did not succeed in getting the money to sign up Kearns."

In Great Falls, "the local committee has demanded that the champion furnish an adequate guaranty that he will appear at Shelby on July 4, in exchange for the posting of the $100,000 now on deposit in Chicago." Walter Eckersall reported that the payment on signing the contract would be the first of three installments and that "if the promoters fail to pay the second . . . Kearns will keep the original $110,000 and can call off the match." That would seem to have made any bond Kearns posted to assure Dempsey's appearance almost a moot point, but he did put up $50,000 for that purpose.

After hundreds of dollars in phone calls and hotel bills, the money seemed to be tied up even more. Molumby "decided to go back to Montana and either get the money released or put on a fight between himself and the Ford Company." He tried to sell Kearns on the idea that the money was, in fact, in the bank, if not as accessible as either of them might have liked.

"Yes," Kearns said, "and there is another hundred million in another bank right across the street but we cannot get it out."

Back in Montana, Molumby insisted, it would take him all of ten minutes to wriggle the cash free from Ford's grip and release it to Kearns. That old soft touch, Kearns said he would sign if Molumby produced just $2,500 in earnest money. Collins would hold the contract in the meantime while Molumby worked to ease the restrictions on the Montana currency. Mayor James A. Johnson received a telegram asking him to supply that placeholding amount himself, and he wired the money to Chicago within three hours.

That financial confusion, combined with Kearns and Kane refusing to be in the same room, made the formality of signing the contract in Chicago a three-day entanglement in itself after weeks of haggling.

"Articles were signed on the fifth of May," Collins said, "and away we rushed to Montana, arriving there on the 8th with $2,500 paid on a $310,000 account."

Even in those stark economic terms, the contract did not figure to be a drain on Shelby's resources at first. Ticket prices were set as high as $50, and the Great Northern Railroad estimated that it would ferry fifty thousand people to Shelby. An arena remained an abstraction two months out, but the only question anyone uttered about it was not, "How?" but rather, "How big?"

There was no hint of a hangover among the investors, who might have sensed they overindulged in their dreams. To the contrary, the party seemed to be in full swing. Not even Molumby, who was later said to be suffering from more than intoxicating ambition, showed any morning-after remorse. "Closing the match was well worth the time and trouble which Collins and myself went to," Molumby said. "I feel sure the Montana business men interested in the venture are satisfied and I am positive they will get their money back. It was a bigger proposition than I anticipated, but now that it is closed I am sure the people of Montana will do everything possible to make it the sporting event of the decade."

Two years after Dempsey-Carpentier drew the famous "Million Dollar Gate," the Montana promoters saw no reason to operate with ambition based on anything less. Any financial concerns were drowned out in the thrill of bold headlines and heady promises. Shelby's brazen frontier spirit spilled into communities around Montana, and, for the moment, the details didn't seem imposing at all. Jack Dempsey was coming.

Nobody felt more grateful for the chance to meet him in person than Tommy Gibbons himself. His end of the deal didn't work out as advertised either. Instead of the $50,000 guarantee offered in the initial reports, Gibbons got almost nothing. A $2,500 stipend covered training expenses, and free use of a home allowed his family to bunk with him in Shelby. Eddie Kane would collect daily admission at his training camp for a few extra bucks, and the exposure would translate into vaudeville paychecks. It did not seem to dismay Gibbons that his income would come, not directly from his labor in the ring, but from whatever other people were willing to pay for his presence. As far as he could tell, the only item of value to him was the heavyweight championship belt. For a journeyman fighter like him, no amount of money could match that.

Once the opportunity of his lifetime became official, Gibbons went on at length in the *Boxing Blade* about how he felt:

I've been trying to get Jack Dempsey into a ring for two years.

Dempsey has been having the time of his life fighting big, heavy elephants that were marks for him, but he'll find I'm a different job on his hands.

I figure I'm about three times as fast as Dempsey. I can take it, and I can come pretty near punching as hard as he can. And that's a combination Dempsey has never been up against.

But I know what I've got and I know what Dempsey's got, though I never put on the gloves with him. I watched him when he trained for the Carpentier fight and I watched him fight. I know I can handle him. Let me have him, that's all I ask.

I figure if Dempsey tries to rush me and I keep out of his way and block some of his blows and give him a few in return, that it will slow him up a bit. He may be able to hit harder than I can but I can hit hard enough to make any of them fall. My idea of how to fight Dempsey is to meet his speed with more speed and give him blow for blow. I can take a lot of punishment and I figure that I can easily connect with him.

Look over his record and you will find that he never fought a real speedy man who could also hit. I have done everything that the public has asked

*of me and have fought better men than he has tackled. I have shown that
I can knock them out.*

*Poor old Willard let Dempsey pile into him without a return. When
he piles into me my legs are good enough to step around a little and I am
quick enough and scientific enough to land some punches of my own.*

*The Carpentier fight proved nothing, as the public has since learned.
Almost any good light heavyweight could have knocked out Carpentier
at the time Dempsey did.*

*All I have got to say is put us in the ring and the public will see a
fight.*

The first sentence would have sufficed: "Just let me at him."

Kearns entered into the agreement with the same salivating ferocity. No matter the outcome, he and Dempsey stood to gain a
financial windfall. Most of the experts polled saw the fight itself
tilted in Dempsey's favor too, despite the almost universal appreciation for Gibbons's style. Everything about the arrangement
satisfied the ample self-interest of Kearns.

Shelby's promoters, meanwhile, found themselves under a
crushing burden. Though they were praised for their courage,
realists around the country recognized the true reason they did it.
Experts in fight promotion also understood the staggering challenge ahead. "Many declared that in their opinion the undertaking is merely an advertising scheme launched for the purpose of
booming the heretofore comparatively unknown Montana town,"
the *New York Times* noted, without naming names. Another column in the *Times* that day suggested that a publicity stunt would
have been the only acceptable reason for choosing this remote
setting for such a big event. "Only on the ground that it has been
arranged for the purpose of advertising Shelby, Mont., can there
be justification for selecting this unknown, little-heard-of, out-
of-the-way spot as the scene for the next world's heavyweight
championship contest."

Of course, it had been done before. Tex Rickard made a lot of money in places like Goldfield and Reno, Nevada, and Toledo, Ohio. "But alongside of the present undertaking these exploitations pale." Even Rickard thought so. And he went on record to express his skepticism.

Rickard noted that he owed much less of a guarantee to the fighters in the Jim Jeffries–Jack Johnson bout in 1910 at Reno. He had a better transportation infrastructure there too, and the fight still attracted only nineteen thousand fans. Gate receipts from Reno would not have come close to covering what the Shelby promoters owed up front. Just four years earlier in Toledo, where Dempsey beat Willard to win the title, the results were much the same.

"I cannot see how the promoters can hope to get a crowd to Shelby which will make the bout a financial success," Rickard said. "And if they do attract the necessary crowd I do not see how they can handle it."

These were not experienced boxing promoters in Montana, but they were gamblers. Mindful of the winnings Rickard realized in Jersey City with the Dempsey-Carpentier "Million Dollar Gate," they were willing to bet their little boomtown that they could do it too. The Broadway producer and former boxing manager William A. Brady, who also doubted that the stunt would succeed, recognized and appreciated that spirit. "You have a boomtown where men are ready to take a chance on anything which promises success," he said, "and I know the men are of the type who would wager a lot of money on the turn of a card."

Shelby had been dealt the hand it wanted. Now the promoters had to play it across the table from a man with the best poker face in the business.

7. The Circus
Comes to Town

With the deal signed, Shelby became the proverbial dog that caught the car. Now what? Trifling details like how to feed and house tens of thousands of expected guests in a town of a few hundred, not to mention where to stage the spectacle that would attract them, took on a certain urgency. Less than two months remained for Shelby to transform itself into the Tulsa of its imagination. Barely six weeks separated the fight's financiers from the due date on the second $100,000 installment owed to Jack Kearns. They needed lumber, labor, lots of money, and more than a little luck. Some liquor would have been nice also, to numb them to the magnitude of what they had done.

The town had almost universal anonymity among the public outside its immediate region. Ranchers and oil men knew of it, but the average citizen of the United States now invited to attend its version of an Independence Day fireworks display would have to do some research before returning an RSVP. Information, respect, reporters, and spectators came in trickles at first, like the first drops from an oil well about to burst. Everybody anticipated a gusher by the time the bell rang. "Shelby may not be near the center of civilization," Tom S. Andrews wrote in his "Timely Ring Gossip" column in the *Boxing Blade*, "but it will surely be on the way proper before the Fourth of July passes into history."

Daydreams about future generations reflecting on this courageous idea that made Shelby prosper into a new Tulsa faded in the face of overwhelming work. An arena existed only on paper, and the promotion of the fight required immediate attention. Urgent though the priorities were, work was slow to begin. Collins established a press bureau almost as soon as he arrived, hiring twenty people to produce informational material for newspapermen around the world. Photographs were also broadcast worldwide. But photographs of what?

Bill Corum of the *New York Times* arrived early, at the behest of a prescient editor hustling him out to cover "the last great fight in the West!" Corum pulled into town on the Great Northern so early, in fact, that it still "resembled a cheap movie set thrown up in the middle of a giant pancake of prairie." A small building advertised itself as FIGHT HEADQUARTERS, with nobody inside, and little else suggested a coming crush of attention and tourists. The Rainbow Hotel's only room with a private bath remained vacant, and Corum became its satisfied but idle occupant, looking for fight news to report, but finding little.

"A week passed and the much talked of arena was still without a location as well as lumber or a contractor to build it," Collins said. "I was beginning to wonder if they were really going to have an arena or not." More of those famous Shelby meetings were held to haggle about where to construct the stadium, a trivial question to Collins under the circumstances but essential to the different factions involved. He urged them to worry more about acquiring the lumber and hiring the labor—details that would have to be done on credit. They had taken that element of the plan for granted, assuming that companies would compete to invest their human capital in the fight with the hope of earning interest on the loan to improve their profit margins. That's not how the companies saw it.

Responses to the initial inquiries gave the promoters the first taste of how cold financial calculations could interfere with their romantic vision. No lumber companies or contractors were willing to take the risk. The possibility of the fight falling through started to percolate again. "Putting it lightly, it was a sad predicament as they presented it to me—$110,000 paid to Dempsey and no place to fight," Collins said. "Now they did not care a whit where the arena was built or how, just so some one would build it."

If their credit was no good, they could at least acquire credibility, which inspired the movement to elect Mayor James A. Johnson as treasurer of the boxing club. Collins recruited him, Johnson accepted, and the club handed him the purse strings. With the money flowing through him and the exclusive authority on how to disburse it, Johnson went to work with typical haste.

"Jim was there like a duck," Collins said. "Steam roller that he is, he gave out notices to all local contractors, including some Great Falls men, to bid on the arena on the following night."

Preliminary work based on the architect's renderings began a few days before the signing of the construction contract, which happened on May 17. J. P. Humphreys of Shelby and B. J. Martin of Billings would share the work. The parties didn't disclose the financial details, but delivery alone of over one million board feet of lumber could not have come cheap. Not to mention the increased costs for materials and labor for three hundred construction workers on a rush job.

Recounting the bid process three months later, Collins reported offers ranging from $66,000 to $99,000. For reasons he did not comprehend, the contract went to one of the higher bids. "I understand the price turned in for the same was about

$84,000," Collins said. "As the accepting of the bid was none of my business, I will not dwell further on the same, but will say that the arena was put up in fast time and also was one of the finest and most up-to-date arenas in the world."

Another facility that could boast of its state-of-the-art grandeur had opened across the country a month earlier. Yankee Stadium hosted its first baseball game for a crowd of 74,200 on April 18, 1923, almost a year after construction began at an estimated cost of $2.5 million. Shelby had just a few weeks and a fraction of the budget for its project. The project organizers only hoped that Jack Dempsey could do for their edifice what Babe Ruth had done in the Bronx. That is, fill the seats.

Jack Dempsey stood on the train platform in Great Falls on the afternoon of May 15 and waved to the welcoming throng. Photographers poised to capture his arrival gave up that objective to protect their equipment from the crush of people jostling for a glimpse. Then the champion stepped down from the platform and seemed to disappear in the mass of humanity. His size set Dempsey apart soon enough, and a path cleared for him and his entourage. A wool cap perched on his head could be seen above most of the people who parted to make room for the broad-shouldered fighter stretching the fabric on his suit as he walked.

That impromptu gathering came together fast as news spread around town that Dempsey would be arriving earlier than expected. He figured to miss a connection in Butte, delaying his arrival until late that night. Will Steege, the manager of the Grand Opera House, happened to be in Butte and wired ahead that Dempsey made the train due in Great Falls in less than two hours. A crowd described in the local paper as the largest ever to greet an arriving train spilled from the platform, across the tracks, and onto the street. Many more tried to approach in cars, but the "scores of automobiles" couldn't creep close enough through all the people for a good view.

Dempsey wended his way to an automobile that became the lead float in a boisterous parade along downtown streets. First, it ferried him two blocks to the Park Hotel, where photographers had found enough room to set up, and the champion dutifully posed with local dignitaries.

Then the municipal band struck up a tune and stepped off ahead of the car, this time with Dempsey on the running board, acknowledging as many of the blurted good wishes as he could with a wave of his beefy hand. From Central Avenue to Sixth Street, then back around to Park Drive and the hotel for more pictures, Great Falls treated Dempsey like royalty.

After he settled into his room at the Park Hotel, Dempsey expressed his appreciation to a *Great Falls Tribune* reporter: "I'm going to like this town. I can see that right now. A man would be hard to please who wouldn't be tickled to death with a reception like that. . . . That was a welcome I'll remember as long as I live—any man would."

Shedding his coat as soon as he entered his room, then rolling up his sleeves with the same restless dispatch, Dempsey displayed "the impatient gesture of an out-of-doors man who is irritated by anything that hampers his movements." Tanned as deeply on his forearms as his face, he looked like a man more familiar with working free of the constraints of starched collars and ties. Gracious in conversation, and boyish in his eagerness to get in the ring, he validated the more benign nicknames bestowed on him. "Gentleman Jack" and "Jack the Kid" didn't carry the inherent menace of the more famous "Manassa Mauler," but they represented indelible parts of his personality. "There's a lot of both about him," the *Great Falls Tribune* reported. "Those who have said the champion is 'just a big boy' didn't say it for publicity purposes alone."

As if to reinforce his image as an outdoorsman, Dempsey went out and bought himself a couple of bulls. He paid $360 for Manly Picture 18 and $290 for Manly Picture 10 at the Montana

Hereford Association auction. With the assistance of the cattle expert Reno Banks, he selected the two purebred bulls and made the highest bids the auction drew that day. Once he bought the bulls, of course, their value skyrocketed in the estimation of other bidders, who offered to take them off his hands before the bow-tied champ even got acquainted with his new acquisitions.

"No, siree!" Dempsey said to any solicitations. "I'm going to keep these boys. They are going right out to my training camp at Great Falls Park." His romance with the outdoors, with the Wild West of his youth, would not be mistaken as a mere element of his championship persona. He meant it.

As an eleven-year-old boy, Dempsey had moved with his family to a hardscrabble ranch in the Colorado village of Uncompahgre. "He rode, fished, and hunted, and became an expert at all. He became a cowboy." Hunting and trapping the coyotes that preyed on the ranch's chickens, lambs, and sheep became part of his rugged education in outdoor self-reliance. Dogs and rabbits were particular favorites. A childhood friend named Susie Osborne said, "He was just a real country boy in them days," and part of that never left him.

Kearns claimed to have indulged his own animalistic interests in Great Falls. "I gathered together a changing menagerie of my own, headed by a corn-haired girl who delighted in imitating Annie Oakley with a six-shooter. As time went on, she became the one and only, because she was really good with that pistol and proficiently frightened off the other available talent."

Shelby had begun to prepare itself for the anticipated crush of visitors with all the hustle it could muster. To the people arriving early, the town brought to mind a boy trying on one of his father's suits. It needed a growth spurt. Toward that end, the town had become a construction site. New loads of labor and lumber rumbled into town on each arriving train, the men and material necessary to build as many as twenty new hotels and rooming houses alone. All in about six weeks. Less than that, really, to make Shelby the least bit accommodating in the days leading up to the fight. For a heavyweight title bout, days likely would turn into weeks of tourists and reporters scouring the town and telegraphing their impressions back home via Western Union.

In mid-May, despite gossip to the contrary, a good meal could be found for seventy-five cents, and the existing hotels still had rooms available at reasonable rates. A new headquarters for the local Chamber of Commerce would open its doors before the end of the month. Offices for the press and public telephone and telegraph services would be located in the building. Built at the intersection of the Roosevelt and Sunshine trails in Shelby, the building also would be the town's showroom, a display case for the charm and growth potential it intended to peddle. "Every person entering the city will be able to get all desired information of the fight, the oil fields and anything with reference to the business and commercial prospects of Montana," the *Great Falls Tribune* reported. Shelby didn't worry about paying for the fight as much as selling itself to captive customers to maximize the return on its investment.

Early returns looked promising. Almost every day, reports of ticket orders from some distant point totaling tens or hundreds of thousands of dollars projected a smashing financial success. Great Falls residents read a headline on May 16 that proclaimed, "Seat Sale Reaches $340,000," which would have paid off Kearns with change to spare. If construction workers felt rushed under their unrelenting deadline, the recently appointed general treasurer, James A. Johnson, must have been relaxed indeed with so much time, money, and tickets left to sell.

Except for the matter of mounting expenses. Predominant among them was the cost of building a stadium out of lumber that had to be shipped into the treeless Shelby landscape. Finishing on time did not concern fight organizers as much as accommodating all the people interested in attending. Plans included a contingency to more than double the size of the proposed arena. "If the seat sale by June 15 warrants it," the *Boxing Blade* reported, "the arena can be increased to a seating capacity of 100,000 by running seats up the natural bowl, one-half mile west of Shelby." The original design accounted for that possibility and used the proximity to the high grassy hills to assure that no spectator, even in the expanded version of the arena, would be more than four hundred and ten feet from the ring. That's a little farther than straightaway center field from home plate in most baseball stadiums.

After some early work had already been completed, local leaders arranged to move the stadium site three-quarters of a mile closer to town. That required a four-hour dismantling and delivery from the old location to the new one. With the Great Northern tracks just a few hundred yards away, the new spot would save time and money in the hauling of lumber from railroad cars to the construction site. Little else changed in the design or the surrounding terrain, although it must not have escaped anyone's notice that the minimum capacity of 100,000 announced only about six weeks earlier had been reduced to 40,000. Too much work to do, and too much excitement in town, made details like that seem minor.

Other items on Shelby's to-do list between May 17 and July 4 included the assembly of ten tanks to store 100,000 gallons of water. That would be only about a ten-day job, increasing the water supply to the town many times beyond its usual capacity. To quench fight-day thirst, pipes then had to be installed to connect the tanks to the stadium.

Up the road from the arena site, a Pittsburgh company went to work on a brick, five-story hotel, which required a pace of about one floor per week to be completed on schedule. "Sleeping has been abolished in Shelby," the *Great Falls Tribune* reported, "and three shifts of eight hours will be used until July 4."

Financial matters came across with more shading, if not outright dishonesty from all sides. Ticket sales were described in hard dollar figures, big numbers from the beginning. This little aside in the *Great Falls Tribune*, then, must have sounded like a warning for interested buyers to hurry up, not an indication of how transactions had been handled to date: "Letters for tickets without money orders or certified checks will receive no attention from the men in charge of the championship battle. Persons wanting tickets are advised that the quicker their money arrives the better the seats they will secure. Prices are from $20–$50. All checks and money orders should be made payable to James A. Johnson, treasurer."

Much as it had for Dempsey, a warm throng greeted Doc Kearns when he disembarked from his train in Great Falls on May 18. A thick knot of self-appointed welcoming committee members overflowed from the platform all the way to Central Avenue. Many of them were massed around Dempsey, who also showed up to meet his manager. It took all of Dempsey's muscle to clear a path for Kearns through the crowd to his waiting car.

"Several hundred automobiles were parked in all available curb space near the station and the resulting traffic jam was a replica of Times Square and Forty-second at high noon." Kearns climbed into his car and rode off as part of another boisterous parade. People lining the route could not get a glimpse of him, so he climbed out and walked with Dempsey, to the delight of the audience.

With Kearns in town to run the camp, Dempsey's training opened with light hiking, rope skipping, and damage to a speed bag. Kearns provided the color commentary as Dempsey went through a slugging exhibition that exhilarated the gathered crowd. His peppering blows ripped the punching bag from the rope holding it to the standard. After a more durable knot held it back in place, Dempsey's next assault loosened the moorings and scattered clattering screws across the pavilion floor. The audience loved it.

In a corral next to the training facility, Manly Picture 18 put on his own snarling display, galloping from end to end within his own "ring." Jerry, a bull pup just seven months old and a new addition to the camp menagerie, watched this display with more trepidation than the crowd safe outside the fence.

Only inanimate opponents got into the ring with Dempsey that day. He treated a dummy with much the same ferocity as the speed bag. Weighted and designed to swing back at Dempsey after a blow, the dummy, "which . . . would knock the average man a half dozen feet," became just another prop to flaunt the champion's panache. After that, he shadowboxed, displaying nimble footwork that awed his fans even more.

Just getting warmed up, Dempsey turned to Kearns with a one-word request for a flesh-and-blood opponent. "Box?"

"No," Kearns said, assuming a paternal trainer's tone.

Sparring would have to wait. Since Dempsey's arrival a few days earlier, his work had been serious but ceremonial. After a couple of more cursory obligations—throwing out the first pitch at a local ball game and attending a luncheon in his honor—he would begin training in earnest.

By then, the free admission offered at the Great Falls park where Dempsey trained would be rescinded. Kearns planned to institute a fee of fifty cents per person, assuring folks it was not for the money but to keep attendance at a reasonable level to maintain order. From Great Falls to Shelby, the curiosity and excitement probably had reached a level feverish enough to justify the crowd-control pricing.

On his first visit to Shelby on May 22, the host town also greeted Kearns as a conquering hero. James A. Johnson, Mike Collins, and hundreds of others welcomed him at the train depot. They repaired to the King Tut dance hall, where they convinced the house musicians to lead them through town to their scheduled banquet. "Saxophones, banjos and drums"—the piano player, alas, could not participate—provided the musical accompaniment to "a fly-infested luncheon at which most of those in attendance wore boots—and pistols," Kearns said.

To the assembled crowd, Kearns tailored his remarks toward what they wanted to hear. "It was a good spot for me to hand out a bit of con," he said. Like his come-on that the Dempsey-Gibbons winner might just return to the Shelby arena on Labor Day to fight Harry Wills: "Shelby is in a position to become the fight capital of the nation."

Kearns could have no more resisted teasing the crowd that way than he could have sworn off oxygen. These people were easy marks who delivered themselves to him, and now they bought every exaggeration and outright lie that passed his lips. "They were eating it up," Kearns said. "Naturally I felt called upon to gild the lily."

If Shelby did not have the makings of a fight capital, perhaps Great Falls would make the region a ring draw. Dan Tracy, the chairman of the boxing commission in Cascade County and a mine and hotel owner from Great Falls, made "an enormous offer" for the champion's next fight. "The figures were not made public," the *Great Falls Tribune* reported, "but Kearns said it was real money just like the Shelby promoters put up for the Dempsey-Gibbons match on July 4."

This may have been more of the lily gilding Kearns referred to in his autobiography, or perhaps both Shelby and Great Falls really would compete for the second heavyweight championship fight in two months to take place in northern Montana. It all might have been a figment of his fertile imagination. Kearns did have difficulty keeping his stories straight. Not that he tried. "Boxing is a business," Kearns said, "and its main stock in trade is the double cross, the run-around and the two-face. In my day a fight manager lived by his wits."

Everything he did was calculated for the audience at hand, designed to maximize his share, often transparent in its pandering, but his genuine charm made it seem natural, from the heart instead of from his . . . wits. Back in Great Falls to stay after his Shelby sales call, Kearns registered at the Rainbow Hotel. He listed "Great Falls" as his residence. Because no detail escaped the reporters covering the fight, they asked him why not New York or Chicago. "Great Falls looks good enough for me; in fact, all of Montana, and I think will register from Shelby, hereafter."

Kearns also noted that Dempsey would be buying a ranch near Great Falls and that he, Kearns, might get a little land of his own and start a livestock business. In a million years, he might never have imagined living in Montana, let alone owning a cattle ranch, but Kearns was never more in his element than under the Big Sky. His big lies were not out of place in that land of wild dreams. Men of action also populated Montana, and they would not have tolerated talk alone for long, but Kearns knew the smoke from his departing locomotive would have wafted away by then.

Shelby now moved to the beat of hammers on wood and other rhythms of a hasty construction schedule. Floodlights were installed at the arena to allow shifts of workers to continue overnight. Schoolhouses were retrofitted, including the installation of "shower baths," to accommodate hundreds of overnight guests who would need a place to stay. James A. Johnson wondered, "What's the use of winding clocks and keeping them in running order. Nobody pays attention to them; there's too much going on."

A labor strike threatened to slow the pace of construction and make the ticking clocks an oppressive presence. Labor leaders posted a new wage scale, demanding $6–$10 a day. Circulars were passed out on the street listing the pay expectations in detail.

The threat lasted only one day. "Two or three [Industrial Workers of the World (iww)] agitators" instigated talk of a strike, leading to a few defections among workers involved in the arena construction and other laborers around town. They were quickly replaced at a rate of sixty cents an hour for a ten-hour day. Chief of Police Alsup himself escorted two of the labor disrupters to the train, and a third made his own way out of town.

On May 25 Dempsey took his first swings at live sparring partners. Gibbons, still on a statewide exhibition tour, had decided only that day to set up his camp in Shelby. It would be a week before the challenger arrived in town to begin his disciplined regimen.

Dempsey looked and felt fresh in his early start, sweating through six rounds against three different opponents on his first day in the ring. Fans paid fifty cents for the privilege of watching from the hillsides around the outdoor camp on a beautiful spring afternoon.

Kearns must have been on to something with his theory of a nominal admission fee as riffraff repellent. A hundred cars surrounded the park, but the audience was as polite as it was large. The *Great Falls Tribune* said: "It must be admitted that everything was much more orderly Thursday than on previous afternoons."

Despite his training head start on Gibbons, Dempsey did not intend to spend the next six weeks in unbroken exertion. This early test of his strength and stamina convinced him that he could allow himself a little of the recreational leisure Montana offered in abundance. "I am going to knock off training next week and go fishing. I don't know where just yet, but I am in good enough shape right now to take the time."

With the vacation still a few days away, Dempsey went through his usual training routine. A windstorm swept blinding swirls of dust through Great Falls on May 25, forcing spectators and participants alike inside the pavilion where a ring had been erected for inclement weather training. Most of the fans went inside as soon as the wind started whipping, but a handful stayed outside just in case, pressing their straw hats tight to their ears, and closing their eyes to the stinging particles.

Dempsey and his partners did not dare venture outside. It became so bad that the doors to the pavilion had to be closed to reduce the dust nuisance. That made the warm air more palatable to breathe, but it did not improve visibility. Light and dust alike were kept out. In the darkness, fans did not watch so much as listen to Dempsey engage his three sparring partners through six rigorous rounds. "It was like listening to a boxing match on the radio," the *Great Falls Tribune* reported. "Slap, crack, thud would go the punches and their success was measured by the resulting grunts."

Most of the slapping, cracking, and thudding came from Dempsey's gloves beating about the heads and bodies of his grunting sparring partners. As referee of the training rounds, Doc Kearns had the best view of his fighter leaving his overmatched opponents quite literally in the dust. Asked whether Dempsey could afford his upcoming week's vacation, Kearns said: "I should say so. He got into condition to go into the ring right now in three days' time. The champion will be in the best condition for this fight that he has ever been. It will do him a lot of good right now to get off into the mountains, fish a little and take a good rest. When he comes back there will still be five weeks left for him to get in the final licks."

Gibbons, meanwhile, continued his state tour, promoting himself and the fight in a series of exhibitions around Montana. When Dempsey left Great Falls to fish, Gibbons came to town to fight. Proving himself a "nimble dodger," he had impressed James Downing, the man in charge of the tour and the matchmaker for the Butte American Legion. Downing overflowed with effusive comparisons to Jim Corbett and Bob Fitzsimmons and called Gibbons "a 30-pound heavier replica of his brother, Mike Gibbons." As effective with his fists as with his feet, Tommy Gibbons raised eyebrows with each powerful jab.

Popular opinion still presumed that Dempsey would win, probably by knockout, but Downing expressed a minority view starting to gain traction: "Dempsey . . . can beat any man he can hit, but if he can not hit Tom Gibbons and Gibbons packs the punch to him after a series of misses, a title may change hands." If anything really could be gleaned from the exhibitions, Gibbons had the potential to follow that script to the letter. He had become his brother's doppelgänger, not just making opponents miss, but driving them to frustration with the skillful way he did it. "There is nothing more disconcerting to a fighter than to miss well-aimed blows." That takes both a mental and a physical toll. After an opportunity wasted, the return blow a well-positioned boxer can deliver layers pain on frustration.

All the hype heaped on Gibbons attracted a large and curious crowd for his Great Falls exhibition at the Grand Theater, the conclusion of the tour. Every seat was filled almost an hour before the preliminary fights, and hundreds of people crammed into standing-room space. They saw for themselves the flitting, physical style writers had gone to such pains to describe. "With that feinting, shifting attack which is peculiar to the Gibbons family and was first developed to its pinnacle by Phantom Mike, Tommy was in and out, standing up all the way, and loosing jarring blows that cracked hard when they landed."

And this was at the end of a grinding ten-day tour by train designed to entertain and energize the locals. Gibbons succeeded in that, even if he depleted his own reserve of enthusiasm in the process. He still had plenty of energy to burn, taking three significant walks, and playing a round of golf on the day of his Great Falls exhibition.

Gibbons also appeared as a guest of the Kiwanis Club of Great Falls, which welcomed him as a representative of Montana's renaissance rooted in its resilient spirit. "Montana has had some long hard years and for a while every one owed every one else," Harold Hoover said in his introductory remarks. "Then last year we had some developments and up in the little town of Shelby, they started pointing at the stars. They picked out the biggest thing that they could get and then they went after it. They got it, the world's championship battle at Shelby."

With "but few words," Gibbons served his verbal tapioca, promising to try his best. He would not have signed on for the fight, he assured the crowd, if he had intended to give anything less. Eddie Kane, assuming the fight manager's key role as spokesman for the strong, silent boxer, went a little further. Tommy Gibbons, he said, "would be the next champion."

Full of rubber chicken and Montana goodwill, Gibbons prepared to shift his focus from exhibition to exertion. After a car trip to Shelby to attend to the final details of his training camp, he would return to St. Paul to collect his wife and children. The entire family planned to be back in Shelby within a week, when training for both fighters would begin in earnest.

Dempsey had a restful but eventful excursion in Montana's scenic wilderness, landing a dozen trout on his first day. The biggest, a two and a half pounder put on display at a Great Falls shop, "was harder and took him longer than almost any of his ring encounters." The heavyweight champion of the world needed more than twenty minutes, or about seven rounds, to defeat the determined trout.

Wading into the river with a rod and reel seemed tame compared to Dempsey's impromptu eagle-hunting excursion. Just over a cliff behind the bungalow where the champion's party bunked, there was an eagle's nest perched on a ledge. Peering through binoculars, Dempsey could see eaglets in the nest. "I sure would like to get one of those young devils," he said.

The camp foreman, Howard Bowman, suddenly regretting that he pointed out the nest to Dempsey, tried to talk him out of the plan he could sense Dempsey hatching. Bowman used the simple logic that, if it could be done, he and his men would already have harvested the eagles. Dempsey did not hear the protests through his own more determined thoughts about how to do it. He concocted a plan. "Bowman listened, frowned and objected," but caution lost. Within fifteen minutes, Bowman and two ranch hands had Dempsey secured with a rope, and he started on his dangerous quest. "The champion was being lowered down the side and three fearful companions were bracing their weights to hold the rope at the top."

THE CIRCUS COMES TO TOWN

As he descended, Dempsey heard Bowman shout a warning from above. The mother eagle had spotted him and, "heading for the nest like a bullet," had the champion in her sights.

"Lower away!" Dempsey shouted, preferring to hasten rather than abort his attempt.

He scooped up one of the young eagles before the mother arrived. She "wheeled and swooped" in pursuit of the kidnapper. Dempsey hit the approaching mother eagle, "and the fight was over." Tucking the captured eagle into his coat pocket, he climbed to the top of the cliff with a new mascot for his camp.

That perilous trip down the sheer face of a Montana cliff to hunt a bird of prey might explain the toll the trip took on Dempsey's trainer, Jerry Lavattas. Dempsey returned to Great Falls in buoyant spirits. Lavattas, responsible for Dempsey's well-being in the ring and out, looked ten years older. "It is especially hard when the champion insists on wading in streams and doing any number of things which aren't at all Jerry's idea of keeping healthy."

To make matters worse, Lavattas let the eagle get away. As he nailed the last slat on the crate to transport it on the train, the eagle pointed its beak at the trainer's hand. The crate toppled, and the eagle escaped into the dense underbrush along the creek.

Shelby, bulking up as fast as possible, could not afford any time away from its appointed tasks, but labor unrest surfaced again. "Carpenters, bricklayers and other union craftsmen walked out of the McCrohan building, in sympathy with the laborers who struck for a day." Some apprehension surfaced in town about an increase in IWW members who might incite extended labor delays. Contractors expressed no such fear, insisting that a dozen men would be available to take the place of any striking worker. "Others have suggested the organization of a vigilante committee," the *Great Falls Tribune* reported, "deputizing every member, giving him authority to carry a weapon and order the Wobblies out of the town, using force if necessary."

Nobody had to resort to physical strike busting. Like the previous threat, this one ended with only a handful of workers walking off the job. More than one hundred reported for work at the arena alone. Construction continued at its necessarily breakneck pace. By May 29 most of the outer edge of the arena had been built to its full height. L. H. Jones, the chairman of the Great Falls Commercial Club, expressed his awe at the speed and quality of the workmanship. "I was surprised at the progress which has been made and the systematic order in which the job is being handled," he said. "The structure will stand as a monument to Montana zeal and determination."

Promoters faced a daunting task of their own in the processing and distribution of tickets for the forty thousand seats in that structure. They had to rubber-stamp all the tickets with government-mandated war tax requirements before they could be sold. Charles Rasmussen, the internal revenue collector from Helena, was in Shelby to oversee the ticket sales on Uncle Sam's behalf. He had a staff of four, expected to increase to ten on the day of the fight, to manage the tax collection on ticket and concession revenue.

Among those concessions would be hamburgers from "what is believed to be a record meat order." An enterprising Shelby concessionaire ordered eight tons of hamburger to be delivered on July 1. That would require the slaughter of thirty-two steers, at an average of five hundred pounds each, and yield meat for an estimated eighty thousand sandwiches. An optimistic entrepreneur, the man intent on cornering Shelby's hamburger market figured that he might have to order even more. As the weeks before the fight passed, he would have considerable competition as the sidewalks filled with purveyors of hot dogs, soft drinks, and other refreshments for the expected masses.

8. Checks and Balances

Tommy Gibbons and his family left St. Paul on June 5 carrying all the good luck the Twin Cities could cram into the luggage compartment. St. Paul mayor Arthur C. Nelson shook his right hand, while Gibbons, dressed for the trip in a three-piece suit and hat, cradled his infant son, Dickie, in his left arm. Among the good-luck charms presented to Gibbons: a flower bouquet shaped like a horseshoe and "a rabbit's foot—killed at midnight under a full moon in an Alabama cemetery." The rabbit's foot came from Mayor Nelson himself. He received it from "a Southern Negro before the last St. Paul election, which resulted in Mr. Nelson's nomination, and [the rabbit's foot] is said to be uncanny in its lucky tendencies."

When Gibbons arrived in Shelby on the Oriental Limited from Saint Paul at 5:30 p.m. June 6, he set off "the greatest excitement the town has known since the railroad came." He participated, with some reticence, in a welcoming ceremony on the train platform featuring all of Shelby's civic heavyweights. To acknowledge the boisterous reception, Gibbons just smiled and waved his hat, preferring to keep the verbal sparring to a minimum for the moment. "I am feeling fine," he said after moving his family into the private home that would be their local living quarters, "but I don't want to begin talking about my fight with Dempsey yet awhile."

Down in Great Falls, Dempsey suffered a cut under unfortunate circumstances. An unknown and overmatched light-heavyweight from Portland, Oregon, named Rocco Stramalgia butted heads with the champion in the ring, reopening a wound around Dempsey's left eye. Blood dripped from the superficial injury. It did not cause serious damage, but the champ would have to be careful to let it heal during the unpredictable training bouts.

Stramalgia disputed the accepted version of events about the cut he inflicted on Dempsey. He said that the intensity of the sparring ramped up after he absorbed a staggering blow. "I caught a hard right smash on the chin and went down, hurt, but not out," Stramalgia said:

I quickly regained my feet and caught Jack napping. He thought I was knocked out cold, and I landed a hard swing to the head and we went into a clinch.

When Kearns separated us, Jack was bleeding from a cut under his eye, and Kearns claimed that I had butted the champion, but I don't think I did.

Stramalgia's opinion did not matter much in that situation, and he disappeared from Dempsey's camp for good.

Despite boxing two more rounds that day with leather headgear protecting his eye, Dempsey chose not to get in the ring for a few days afterward. Plaster and cotton covered the slight swelling of his eyelid the next day, but the injury did not concern him, and he remained in his usual good spirits.

Worse for Dempsey, he had to let his coyote go. The most menacing animal among his mascots, it "snapped at everybody and left its teeth impressions in several camp attendants." Unable to control the coyote, Dempsey turned it loose toward the western hills, where it disappeared in the distance.

Two wolfhounds remained, among many other animals wild and domesticated, and Dempsey relished mingling with fans and playing ball with the dogs. The idle time also gave him an opportunity to display his card tricks, which became quite a camp phenomenon.

Gibbons set out for his first training hike in Shelby on June 7, planning to walk four or five miles. He "covered sixteen instead," the *New York Times* reported, "most of it at a trot and finished as fresh as if he had just walked around the block." Reporters and photographers followed in a car, where the sparring partner Buck Pape retired when the roadwork became too grueling for him. Another training companion, Bud Gorman, went the extended distance with Gibbons, eight miles south to the winding Marias River and back. Physical conditioning would not be a concern for Gibbons with almost a month to train before the fight.

Mental preparation also occupied the time. Not long before embarking on his quest for a championship, Gibbons became a student of the sport. Literally. A clinic at the University of Minnesota taught him the scientific aspects of the sweet science. "I have tried to learn all I could about nerve centres," he said. "It is easier to knock a man out scientifically than by brute force. It's simply a matter of pressing the right buttons and the lights go out."

Hills rose like stair steps from Shelby's main street up to a plateau where hikers like Gibbons could cross an expanse of grass and descend to the Marias River on the other side. Up just a step or two from the center of town, the Gibbons family settled into the donated "Robinson home, on a knoll about a quarter of a mile from the arena." It was a nine-room house, but the Gibbons family had it to themselves. Sparring partners and other training camp personnel slept in tents pitched on the expansive lawn.

The wooden stadium, under rush construction, could be seen down the incline from the front porch of the "Gibbons Green Gable." A steady stream of sightseers passed the home, hoping for a glimpse of the challenger, but he was busy working somewhere between there and the river. Five-year-old Tommy Jr. and three-year-old Jack provided entertainment enough in their cowboy and Indian costumes. Their baby brother, Dick, watched it all from his carriage.

Other than the weakness for vanilla ice cream that he continued to indulge, Gibbons ate only what his camp chef from St. Paul (his wife, Helen) prepared. He could wash it down with a swig from a five-gallon bottle of "mountain spring water" the family received every day from Glacier Park. The label read: "This gives Tom Gibbons the punch."

Always the strong, silent type, Gibbons began to engage in some verbal sparring with Dempsey. Both fighters contributed daily columns to the *Minneapolis Tribune*, meant to be firsthand updates and behind-the-scenes accounts of their training routines. A reader could be forgiven for presuming that these were ghostwritten dispatches—and the competing *Minneapolis Journal* suggested as much in a wry ongoing satire of the battle for a literary knockout. But their bylines appeared every day, giving voice to the fighters in the only way possible during an era before talk-radio posturing and staged press conferences.

Gibbons talked trash. His initial offering on June 12 set the tone for his journalistic motif: diminishing the myth of Jack Dempsey. He went point by point:

(1) *Dempsey is great only against big, slow moving giants, whose bodies furnish such a huge target that a blind man could hit them.*

(2) *Dempsey never put away a single opponent who was clever and a hitter at the same time, except Carpentier, and the world knows that the*

Frenchman had a tin chin. . . . What's Dempsey's reputation built upon?
It is anything other than that he put away Fre[d] Fulton, Oil Morris, Jess
Willard and a lot of other has-beens or joke performers?

Across the page from that attack on his record and reputation, Dempsey demurred. He took pains to prop up Gibbons—with a by-the-numbers construction readers might have recognized from just a few columns over—as a model of toughness and a true threat to his title:

In all honesty and in all seriousness I want to say that I look forward to the
Gibbons battle with an idea that it will be the toughest of my career. . . .
    Just why some folks think Gibbons is going to be soft is a puzzle to me.
Here's a man as follows:
    (1) Never been knocked out.
    (2) Never been knocked down.
    (3) Is about as tall as I am and almost as heavy.
    (4) Is regarded as the fastest, cleverest heavyweight in the ring har-
        ness today.
    (5) Has knocked out something like 30 of the last 34 he has fought.
        And yet some call him soft!

When the famous sports writers began to arrive, young Bill Corum of the *New York Times* lost his private bathroom privileges at the Rainbow Hotel. He relinquished the tub for a good cause. William O. McGeehan, the *New York Herald* writer known as "Sheriff," needed it to keep the beer cold for the working press assigned to the dry town.

Corum ended up down the hall with a roommate he remembered well, if only by his first name, Phil, a bartender from St. Paul and a friend of Gibbons's manager, Eddie Kane. Phil was a generous man who brought a suitcase stocked with pints of whiskey that he shared with Corum and anyone else who wanted a sip without charge or limit.

The downside to the arrangement was that, in the double bed he shared with Corum, Phil slept with a lit cigar clenched between his teeth. "When he snored, the exhalation sent sparks and ashes flying up like a Roman candle on the Fourth of July. Naturally, this made sleeping hazardous, in fact impossible." Try as Corum might to suggest he should stub that stogie out before falling asleep, Phil continued his lifelong habit. "Nothin's happened yet," he said.

Unsettling things were happening around town. While Dempsey took his first day off from sparring to allow the cut over his eye to heal, Toole County authorities initiated a sweep of Shelby. Montana attorney general W. D. Rankin informed Loy Molumby that "moral conditions" must prevail at Shelby. That meant no gambling and, in the era of Prohibition, no liquor. No less than the mayor of Shelby, James A. Johnson, knew his way around a card table pretty well, and the town did not lack outlets for other vices. The national attraction of a heavyweight championship fight also figured to lure freelance profiteers without much concern for the laws on the books, local, state, or federal. To prevent all that, Shelby law enforcement officials took preventative measures "to keep the town free of the tough element."

Sheriff H. E. Benjamin advised Rankin that "a number of arrests were made . . . and men without visible means of support and undesirable women told to leave town within 24 hours." They wanted their town to be free of anything objectionable as it spruced up for the expected influx of people purchasing tickets from coast to coast.

An early morning raid of the Chicken Shack, where local and federal officers confiscated alcohol and made two arrests, was "the beginning of the end for the bootlegger and operator of resorts" in town. Other disturbances of the peace were more violent, and just as lawless, despite less police attention.

Outside a local hotel, a fight between a man and a woman awakened several guests. From their windows, they witnessed "the man swing a left and hit the woman under the eye, knocking her a distance of about 20 feet, where she fell in the mud." That prompted another man to yell from the hotel that he would come down there and give him the same treatment. When the man on the street promised to come up to his room instead, the gallant gentleman from the hotel window reconsidered. "The fighter failed to find the room in question and quiet was again resumed."

He almost did find the room and raised even more of a ruckus in trying. The threat from above came from Bill Corum's cigar-chomping roommate Phil. Corum, not inclined to fight, pushed the dresser and chair against the door and prepared to exit by the window if it came to that.

"Ossified as a hoot owl," the cowboy tried to break into the vacant room next door. Anybody who had not been awakened by the tussle on the street was now up and curious. That included the hotel manager, who summoned the sheriff, who released the cowboy into the custody of the woman he hit. "As always happens, she rushed into his arms and pleaded with the law not to put him in the pokey," Corum said. "She won her case."

Phil, meanwhile, emerged from under the bed, where he insisted he had not been hiding, just looking for the cigar that rolled under there in the commotion. Like the love between the cowboy and his battered lady friend, it was still burning, much to Corum's dismay. "That damned inextinguishable cheroot still was glowing and throwing off its usual sparks."

Not far from that ugly incident, "in a shack on the north side of town," a local chef took a bullet in the calf. William Warwick told the *Great Falls Tribune* he was asleep when a masked intruder shouted, "Stick 'em up!" Witnesses said the shooting followed an argument over a woman.

Yet another man named John Lucas suffered "several painful knife wounds" in a separate incident around the Black Cat cabaret. He did not identify who had stabbed him, and, as with the other two physical confrontations that violent night, officers took no report and made no arrests.

There was, however, apparent police activity inside that establishment. Patrons at the Black Cat could find an ample selection of potential companionship as "10 or 15 ladies, oh, extremely wildish, fought for the privilege of a dance with you." The intrepid and inspired satirist Richard Henry Little of the *Chicago Tribune* noted that the dance-card shuffle did not last: "Somebody replevined the bar and the tables and the gas fixtures and the cash registers and everything except the wildish ladies."

Still, all those reports only fueled the impression of Shelby as a town out of control. Sheriff Benjamin disputed that notion and cited thorough investigations of complaints and thwarted attempts to import and operate "gambling devices" in Shelby as proof to the contrary. Officers could not confiscate the machines until they were used, but Benjamin knew what he would do with them if that occurred. "We haven't much in the way of jail facilities," he said, "but the Marias [R]iver will hold many slot machines and roulette wheels if they ever attempt to operate them."

Another raid, at a "gay party" almost thirty miles from town, emphasized the federal support local authorities would have in their mission. Agents took two dozen people into custody, confiscated liquor, and arrested the supplier, identified as Jack Walton, who was fined $150 for his alleged Prohibition violation.

Deputies patrolled roads into Shelby, refuting rumors of whiskey flowing into town by the carload. Within the town limits, both the Chicken Shack and a dance hall called Days of 49 painted over their signs at the request of officers on the alcohol beat. A *Great Falls Tribune* reporter went undercover to take a deeper look into the liquor and gambling trade in town. He heard only, "Nothing doing," from proprietors all over Shelby. Owners of a raided establishment, a den of suspicion, put their business up for sale at a cut rate. Along with the repeated denial of service, that fire sale served as evidence that the law won and satisfied the newspaper that "Shelby is a closed town."

On a trip to drum up ticket sales, Mayor Johnson and Mike Collins took offense at the attorney general's public posturing. "This is due to some one wanting to get his name in the paper," Collins said. Johnson just shrugged it off, insisting that drinking in Shelby was not a significant problem. Not long before, the mayor noted, the state's Prohibition officer and an assistant investigated rumors for four days and found nothing of consequence.

There were plenty of places to eat, dance, and even drink—at least sodas. The combination of the previous year's oil strike and now the fight prompted close to two dozen new dance halls to open in Shelby. Entertainment options were plentiful, most notably the musical stylings of Patricia Salmon. Her "talents" attracted the attention of New York reporters, whose effusive reviews compelled Florenz Ziegfeld to offer her a part in his Follies.

"Hair-tinted and beauty-lotioned, she was not a bad looking girl, but she could not dance, sing or act," Bill Corum wrote. "However, she could yodel, which wouldn't have been so bad if she had yodeled well."

Still nursing the cut over his eye, Dempsey spent a day casting flies on the Missouri River. Fans caught only a brief glimpse of him in white flannels as he, Doc Kearns, and Mike Trant, a Chicago detective who provided security for the champ, carried their fishing tackle to a rowboat and prepared to "depopulate the Missouri." A full weekend of workouts awaited in the coming days, before one more fishing diversion and then total focus on the July 4 fight. Seeking a positive spin on the minor nuisance of an injury that idled Dempsey, the camp members described it as a "blessing in disguise." The cut—which, it turned out, required two stitches—forced the restless Dempsey to relax with almost a month left before the fight, rather than sharpening himself too much, too soon.

On his second day traversing the Shelby terrain, Gibbons altered his routine to simulate the particular rigors of a fifteen-round fight. He ran for three minutes, then walked for one, and so on, following the intervals of the ring. Then he and members of his entourage went gopher hunting.

It was a tedious pursuit, more like a police stakeout than a sportsman's quest. With guns at the ready, they waited, and waited, careful not to let their minds wander because they had only an instant to fire when a gopher popped up through his hole. "The Gibbons party boasted of its success, but it brought no trophies of the hunt."

The sun baked Dempsey's outdoor camp when he returned to training Saturday afternoon, June 9. He honed his quickness on the speed bag, sparing it the punishment that had sent it tumbling to the ground in previous sessions. Against the heavy bag, however, "he got down to the savage crouch and started shooting out the vicious wallops." Dempsey tore a hole in that bag with his thunderous body blows, causing its guts to spill out on the ground. His own open wound over his eye had not yet healed enough to risk sparring, but Dempsey worked himself into a dripping sweat anyway.

Mike Collins announced the next day in Spokane, Washington, that ticket orders had reached $450,000, including a new request from New York for 200 seats. That came from the Great Northern Railroad official E. T. Ryan, who wanted the premium $50 tickets for his party, which planned to depart July 1 by special train. Another order for 250 ringside seats arrived from Los Angeles. Mayor Johnson, traveling with Collins on a promotional barnstorming tour, echoed the assurance of the sheriff that visitors had nothing to fear in Shelby. "There will be no riot of gambling and drinking or pickpocketing," he said. "We have a squad of special detectives meeting every train and requesting every suspicious character to move on. Besides, every businessman and every employee is a special officer." To readers of the *New York*

Times, Shelby sounded like nothing less than a police state where the only hint of danger would be in the ring.

As a center of commerce, the town also started to provide a few goods and services to early arriving tourists at a considerable markup. "Shelby's first honest-to-goodness big town soda fountain was installed today and now it is possible to buy the ordinary 5-cent drink for a quarter. There is no time for small change here. There are no pennies, but the lack of these is offset by a plentiful supply of nice big silver dollars. Many a man is accused of carrying a gun in Shelby when, as a matter of fact, he had only a 10-dollar bill changed." No question that money, or the lack of it, would cause more apprehension around the state over the next month than any six-shooter.

Business instincts of nickel-and-dime merchants setting up shop in Shelby exceeded the common sense the region's banking and oil barons showed in selling the fight. If, in fact, close to a half million dollars worth of tickets had been sold by June 8, the financial health of the event would have been "in the pink," like Gibbons after his long walk. Whatever truth that financial proclamation included, it misrepresented a much more ominous reality. Promoters owed Kearns his second $100,000 installment within a week, and their balance sheet did not offer comfort that they could meet the deadline. They told Kearns not to worry, that they had $80,000 earmarked for him already with the rest assured by the deadline of midnight, June 15.

Behind the scenes, they were not so confident. Plenty of ticket orders had arrived, but most did not include so much as a deposit, let alone payment in full. People were interested, but they preferred to make reservations and pay later in person. That created a significant cash-flow problem despite such a significant amount of tickets "sold."

For the enterprise to have any hope of success, the promoters needed Kearns to assure the press that Dempsey would fight. Only that could convince the public and assure enough cash on the barrelhead to cover all the expenses. In a meeting with the senior fight officials, Kearns vowed that he "would so state to the newspapers if the second payment was made." In a place and time Body Johnson remembered as the end of the Old West, a handshake sufficed as a binding agreement among the business-men of Montana's high plains. It meant something else to Kearns, whose fingers were still sticky from the Klondike. Jim Speer, a Great Falls judge and one of the promoters, did not want the man with the molasses fingerprints to touch any money until Dempsey stepped in the ring. Speer advised James A. Johnson to that effect with Kearns in the room.

"Jim, I don't trust this bastard and I advise you to keep the money until the day of the fight," Speer said. "If he keeps his word he will get it, if not, we can sue him for everything he's got."

In support of Speer, an attorney from Livingston named Kelly, who attended the meeting as an adviser to Molumby, decided the threat of hand-to-hand combat might be better motivation for Kearns than a mere handshake. "O.K. you tinhorn S.O.B. you used to be a pug, either you agree with Judge Speer or else step out in the alley and we will see who comes back."

Surveying Kelly, an ex-all-American football player from the University of Montana, "Kearns didn't want any part of it." He agreed to make a definitive statement about the fight, on pay-ment of the second installment, and the promoters took him at his word. "They just couldn't believe," Body Johnson said, "that anyone could be the liar that Kearns turned out to be."

Three days before the second installment was due, Body John-son, Molumby, and Major Gene Lane continued barnstorming the state in Earl Vance's plane to drum up ticket sales. They climbed aboard around 6:15 a.m. on June 12 in Livingston, bound for Butte. Shifting winds forced Vance to abort two attempts to take off, but he chugged off the ground on his third try. Seconds after the wheels cleared the field, a crosswind caught the wings of the plane, traveling seventy miles an hour at an altitude of only twenty-five feet, and tilted it east toward a telephone line. Its right wing and landing apparatus clipped the wire, and the plane plummeted to the ground. Vance, who suffered only a cut on his jaw, wrested himself from the wreckage, cut off the electricity to prevent a fire, and pulled out his passengers. They were unconscious. Body Johnson suffered the most serious injuries, arriving at the hospital feeling "more dead than alive," but they were not life threatening. A compound fracture of his right arm and bruises around his face and body left him laid up in Livingston for several days. Molumby, with a sprained shoulder and back, continued the promotional tour on his own, by train.

The accident created more chaos at the Shelby headquarters, which already "could be described as a hypothyroid mess." Expenses were mounting, investors were restless, and the difference between public pronouncements of sales figures and actual income was, to paraphrase Mark Twain, the difference between lightning and a lightning bug.

While Molumby labored to sell tickets alone, the nation's most notorious gate-crasher, "One-Eyed" Connelly, showed up in Great Falls. "The fight's official now," Connelly said. "I'm here." He turned up everywhere, most recently at the Kentucky Derby and the Indianapolis 500, before making his way west to Montana.

Connelly had become such a fixture at big events that he didn't have to sneak in; the organizers usually found him some sort of ghost employment suited to a passing apparition. "I don't know what I shall do at this fight," he said. "Sometimes I am guardian over the ring; sometimes I take care of the press box." In Connelly's mind, his presence validated an event, but he just added another layer to the surreal atmosphere around Shelby.

The leader of the Anti-Saloon League of Montana also made an appearance to support the enforcement of Prohibition laws and prevent Shelby from becoming "a wild and wooly town."

The Reverend Joseph Pope echoed Attorney General Rankin's insistence that local officials enforce the letter of the law or put the fight and their jobs at risk.

Not far from the Gibbons camp, a five-foot rattlesnake suffered a fatal blow at the hands of Shelby resident Chester Armstrong. It had eight rattles, which became collector's items at fight headquarters, where "there was a wild scramble for souvenir." The idea of snake hunting intrigued Gibbons enough that he let the gophers be for one day and went in search of his own trophy rattler.

Reverend Pope of the Anti-Saloon League offered a wry aside that nobody should worry about being bitten. "I am informed that there is plenty of snake poison remedy in Shelby or close by," he said, "so a snake bite should not bother anybody."

Between the plane crash, the arrival of a fan famous for wrangling free admission, and the unsettling hiss of rattlers, the fight achieved omen overload as the deadline for the second installment loomed.

Despite the jostling of bodies in the air and on the ground, Shelby had developed a placid, if rapid, pace of evolution toward its Independence Day destiny. Construction of the stadium proceeded ahead of schedule, and the Great Northern Railroad continued to add extra skeleton tracks to accommodate the special trains expected.

As if providing a dress rehearsal for July 4, many tourists passed through Shelby on their way to Glacier National Park. "All of the sightseers stop over in Shelby awhile, and many of them expect to return in time for the big fireworks on the Fourth. On that day it looks as if Shelby will be where the West begins and ends," the New York Times reported. Its support for this thesis involved, not just the travelers passing through the town's figurative turnstiles, but that finally a day passed without either debris or debates about debauchery. "There were no airplane accidents or visits by State officials to stir the town."

Just when it appeared to the public that Shelby might be outgrowing its awkward promotional adolescence, the truth about its excessive exuberance started to leak. It began with a vague report of "pessimism" from Great Falls that the promoters could afford the second $100,000 installment to Kearns. Denials and "declarations of a heavy advance sale" from the promoters were loud and clear, if not convincing to people in a position to know better. Doubt started to seep through the cracks in Shelby's financial facade.

Kearns prepared to board a train in Great Falls on June 14 for a ride to Shelby, where he expected to receive his second check. James A. Johnson and a delegation of promoters stopped him. Their transaction would be consummated in Great Falls instead, they informed him, and Kearns said that the group assured him it would be paid on time and in full. "This does much to dispel an undercurrent of rumor that the money was not in hand and could not be paid," the *Great Falls Tribune* reported. That reassuring news appeared next to the first published photograph of Vance's mangled plane. A destructive shift in the winds of public opinion would leave the fight promotion in a similar condition come midnight, June 15.

When that witching hour arrived, the sheepish Shelby backers had to inform Kearns of the truth. They had only $1,600 for him. "That day of reckoning found them approximately 98 percent short," John Lardner wrote in his classic story for the *New Yorker* recounting the elaborate game of financial charades in Shelby.

"Well, that's a hell of a note," Kearns said. "But, as I told you when we signed for the fight, if the terms aren't met, no fight."

Johnson offered livestock, fifty thousand head of sheep to be precise, to cover the outstanding bill.

"Now just what the hell would I do with 50,000 sheep in a New York apartment?"

George H. Stanton, the president of the Stanton Trust and Savings Bank and another of the many interested "promoters," suggested giving the fight itself to Kearns.

"Why don't you take over the promotion and ticket sale?" he said. "From all I can see, you own the fight right now."

"Damned if I'll promote it. These guys are the promoters. I'm trying to train a fighter. Just let them get up the money or there won't be any fight. That's all I've got to say."

That "undercurrent of rumor" surfaced in boldface facts that spilled from the sports section to the front pages from Great Falls to New York. Kearns emerged from a meeting after midnight furious about the situation as he now understood it. Lumber for the arena had been mortgaged, leaving that end of the enterprise $60,000–$80,000 in debt. Many of those supposed advance ticket orders had been received without payment, putting the fight in such financial duress that the *New York Times* reported on its front page that it might be off. That news figured to choke off the trickle of ticket sales even more.

Adding a thick layer of irony to the proceedings, Kearns took offense that the fight backers hadn't trusted him with the truth. "He asserted that he would have been prepared to agree to any reasonable arrangement in an emergency if he had been taken into the confidence of those who were aware of the existing conditions."

Those conditions prompted new ownership to assume control of the fight. Stanton ultimately rallied a group of businessmen to provide $77,000 of the necessary funds in an eleventh-hour drive to pay the second installment to Kearns. James A. Johnson contributed $50,000 of it himself.

Kearns received his payment late, but in full, at 5:15 p.m. on June 16 and dropped the threat of calling off the fight. In public, however, he carefully avoided definitive statements, leaving open the escape loophole and his leverage for the third installment.

In return for their generous ante that allowed the bout to live to play another hand, the businessmen demanded to put their organizational currency behind it too. They insisted on installing Dan Tracy, who had made his money in mining and owned part of the Park Hotel in Great Falls, as the acting director. Molumby, Collins, and Mayor Johnson all remained active in the promotional and financial details, but Tracy assumed much more than superficial control. As a condition of accepting the job, he received assurances that his power would be absolute.

"I want it thoroughly understood from this moment on that I am to be the boss of the whole business and the only boss," Tracy said. "I have been induced to assume the position as leader of this affair against my better counsel—not because I am apprehensive of the success of the bout, but because of my lack of familiarity with boxing promotion. It is to be understood that I am to have a free hand in directing things. If I want to go to Shelby and revise any plans I will do it. If I want to hire or fire anybody I will do so. If I want to clean house entirely I will do it if circumstances warrant. In other words, I am to be the head of this affair in fact as well as in fancy and I am to treat circumstances and conditions as my judgment dictates and as I encounter them. . . . I will lay my cards face up on the table. I can do no more."

While Tracy tried to create transparency and restore economic order to an enterprise in disarray, the principal participants in the athletic end of it worked without any apparent concern about cancellation. After a brief break that included a side trip to Glacier National Park, Gibbons resumed training on June 16 with notable intensity. After his usual eight-mile run at dawn, he jumped rope and worked a heavy bag under a blistering afternoon sun. Thus lathered, he went eight rounds with three different sparring partners, including a new addition to his entourage who stirred some excitement from the three hundred curious spectators. Jimmy Delaney looked impressive in a recent fight against light heavyweight champion, Gene Tunney. Displaying the slippery traits of his manager, Mike Gibbons, Delaney turned his two rounds into "the fastest and most scientific boxing so far seen in the Gibbons camp." Missing with the left he had landed all along, Gibbons struggled to apply his customary sting, but "his footwork and elusiveness along the ropes pleased the crowd immensely."

Back in Great Falls, where the financial punishment forced the fight itself to take a standing-eight count, Dempsey continued bludgeoning whoever dared to enter the ring with him. "Mauled" them, according to the *New York Times*. For a few days, at least, his repertoire appeared to match his reputation, and he impressed the skeptical spectators. "He hit more accurately and with greater power back of his blows; he was faster; his defense was almost airtight and his wind was excellent."

A new sparring partner showed up in the Gibbons camp with the experience to provide the most informed analysis available of the two fighters. Rocco Stramalgia, who was excused from Dempsey's stable after the incident that bloodied the champion, went a few rounds with Gibbons.

Nobody else could offer the firsthand perspective of the fighters' respective skill and conditioning less than a month before the bout. Stramalgia echoed the popular opinion of Dempsey as a dangerous slugger with a knockout punch always cocked and loaded. He also supported another theme creeping into the cognoscenti's consciousness: Gibbons could neutralize that power with the cumulative effect of his precision.

"Dempsey hit me harder," Stramalgia said, "but Tom landed on me twice as often. . . . When it comes to landing on them, I found Gibbons about three times as hard to hit as Dempsey. In fact, I was dizzy from missing punches aimed at Tom."

Mike Collins, now known to all as the matchmaker in the uneasy Shelby shotgun wedding of Doc Kearns and Eddie Kane, turned the *Boxing Blade* into nothing less than a publicity brochure for the fight. Of course, it would have been the magazine's main story for months no matter the circumstances or his relation to them. From respectable daily newspapers to the salacious *National Police Gazette*, every publication concerned about its circulation included considerable Dempsey-Gibbons coverage. But Collins had incentive to sell the fight, not just report on it, and the *Boxing Blade* did its best to maintain public confidence amid increasing doubt.

Just as the devastating financial news began to break, the June 16 issue sounded a little more pleading and desperate in its pitch. A week after assuring readers that vices would be toned down in a town with a wild, Old West reputation, lubricated with oil money and rumored rum running, the *Blade* now highlighted Shelby's rowdy side:

The one o'clock closing law is nix in this boom town. Proprietors of places of amusement, after a meeting, marched solemnly to the site of the arena west of the town, buried the keys of their places on the spot where the Dempsey-Gibbons ring will be erected. Shelby is wide open as regards late hours. The cabarets wheeze out their more or less tuneful music until it is time for the morning train from the Coast. Then the stragglers who can't seem to be able to go to bed until they are sure the sun is shining again, wander down to the depot and eye the transcontinental travelers. Jazz climbs on the throne early in the evening. As soon as the east bound train has slipped away over the flats, the pleasure palaces come into their own. The sheik-like orchestra from the King Tut dance pavilion competes for popularity with the cowboy trio grinding out alleged music on homemade instruments at The Mustang. The boys just in from the oil fields for a little recreation swarm to the dance halls. A lone movie does its best to attract, but the competition is too keen. Hectic Shelby hasn't time to sit for an hour in a picture house.

A movie could not compare to the real-life drama building to a crescendo with two weeks until the fight. From the fighters to famous newspapermen like Grantland Rice and Damon Runyon, the Hi-Line became the setting for a cautionary tale about big dreams in a small town, and the hustlers who will happily take advantage. Optimism about the fight resurfaced soon enough, but it must have sounded like fiction to discerning readers after the flop sweat Shelby experienced over the second installment payment.

As his first order of business, Dan Tracy traveled to Shelby to evaluate the leadership and structural integrity within the fight's main office. He brought Frank Fogerty from Great Falls as his top assistant but otherwise made no changes at the top. After his preliminary review of the situation, Tracy pronounced himself satisfied and pledged to raise the final $100,000 installment with due speed to avoid another tense encounter with cancellation. Aside from his resolute belief in himself to alter the status quo, he offered the public no specifics about how he would do that. A *New York Times* headline that read "Tracy Expresses Confidence After Conference with His Assistants" would have to suffice as assurance to prospective paying customers.

James A. Johnson, Kearns, Collins, and the array of businessmen and their representatives from around Montana continued their financial scuffling in private. There was little, if any, improvement in the fight's bottom line. Despite a combination of silence, delaying tactics, and false optimism in public, the promoters could not deny the facts staring them in the face. Tracy could not even unearth satisfactory facts to plot a course of action. There were hundreds of thousands of dollars in tickets "sold" but no sign of the money. His frustration about this festered for days while all seemed quiet on the economic front.

Once Kearns received the second installment, the promoters expected him to put any lingering speculation to rest with a statement that the fight would go on as planned. He hedged, expressing only his "confidence" that they would come through with the final $100,000 they owed him. "Kearns would say one thing inside the room, then he'd go outside and say another," Body Johnson said. "He would lie like hell and he did it time after time."

His slippery tactics notwithstanding, Kearns did have a contract with the promoters and the right to hold them to it. They had agreed to reasonable, if untenable, terms. The irony is that, if

Kearns had only done a little selling on Shelby's behalf, if he had promised the press in no uncertain terms that the fight would go on, if he had taken to "gilding the lily" just a little about the oil boomtown's attractions, he and everybody else probably would have fared better in the end.

9. Under Water

Ballyhoo for the bout resumed soon after Dan Tracy assumed
authority in Shelby. He left the office about three o'clock on his
first day in town to watch Gibbons spar. Kearns "graciously declined" Eddie Kane's offer to take a peek at the challenger, but
James A. Johnson and Mike Collins accompanied Tracy in poking
around that part of their investment. Interested spectators could
gather around the training ring and examine the physical, if not
fiscal, aspects of the fight for themselves. Among the crowd that
day, high rollers like the Great Northern Railroad executive W. P.
Kenney and more than a dozen of his associates watched with
a skeptical eye. From that ringside perspective it looked like a
solvent enterprise, a competition worth the price of admission.

They had seen Dempsey demonstrate his considerable power
already—enough power to doubt that Gibbons could give him
much of a fight. Among the other problems hovering over the

match like the dark clouds gathering over Shelby, the prospect of a quick knockout did not figure to generate much train traffic to the middle of nowhere. Gibbons reassured them, with the assistance of the newsmen reporting his prowess, that special trains might be necessary after all. He pushed around well-regarded heavyweight Bud Gorman for two rounds in an aggressive scrap that delighted raucous spectators. Jimmy Delaney went a couple of rowdy rounds with him too before the talkative Tillis Herman took his turn.

A Mexican welterweight with the stated ambition "to be the first man to ever topple Gibbons off his feet," Herman set out to prove he meant it. Showing the well-heeled visitors what Rocco Stramalgia discovered, Gibbons did not succumb to Herman's onslaught. "His blows just would not go where he aimed them," a testament to the footwork that gave Gibbons a fighting chance.

"It is boxers of the Herman type that Gibbons needs just now, men who will wade in and mix things with him. If the future may be forecast from the past there will be no hesitancy on the part of Dempsey when the gong sounds on the Fourth," the *New York Times* reported. "As some one remarked today, Kane should put two or three men of Gibbons' sparring mates in the ring at the same time if he wants Tommy to be accustomed to the sort of attack he is going to have to face when the champion opens fire."

Taking them one at a time, Gibbons danced around waves of Dempseyesque fury, displaying enough power in the process to impress the important people watching. When the bell sounded concluding his last round against Herman, Gibbons was smiling along with the crowd he had entertained.

That fast, news from Shelby shifted back to boxing. The shaky business situation was treated like a hiccup that had passed—at least in public. The scare the promoters experienced did not, by any means, cure their persistent case of financial hiccups. It just managed to stifle them for a while.

Gibbons, or at least the ghostwriter composing his columns, continued to talk the talk about how he would stare straight into Dempsey's intimidating glare until the champion blinked. Or, rather, until Dempsey's eyes were swollen shut:

I rather like his face, and I certainly shall enjoy looking at it on July 4th. But I find it has a few defects. I will want to remedy them. I think his nose is a little too narrow. It should be flatter to bring out the full beauty of his facial contour. I shall try to flatten that nose to the right shape.

His eyes are good eyes; but I think they are a bit too drab—that is [the] color scheme around them. I think that the application of a little black and a little blue around each would add wonderfully to his appearance. I'll do that beautifying for Jack, too—and I won't charge him a dollar for the work.

Fight details dominated reports from the training camps in Shelby and Great Falls. As if to foreshadow the storm to come, rain settled over the region on June 19, disrupting only training routines for the time being. But no image better captured the mood and misfortune of the Hi-Line in the apprehensive weeks leading up to July 4, 1923, than those storm clouds. A drought had ravaged Montana's agricultural economy for the previous six years, but now the heavens opened, muddying the dirt roads into town, further complicating travel to a remote location.

Dempsey ignored the dawn-to-dusk downpour on June 19 despite a cold. He boxed ten rounds with an emphasis on his defensive tactics. His sparring partner, Jack Burke, found the same blind spot Mike and Tommy Gibbons identified in the pictures they studied. During an otherwise impressive display of bobbing and weaving, Dempsey's weakness allowed Burke to land a driving left to the stomach. "This blow is a favorite of Gibbons, who is much faster than Burke and a more accurate hitter." Those fleeting glimpses of rust and vulnerability from the champion with an invincible reputation created some doubt about the outcome. A grudging public began to believe Gibbons had a chance.

The tale of the tape revealed Dempsey and Gibbons to be the most evenly matched competitors ever in a heavyweight championship fight. A *New York Times* analysis depicted Dempsey as three quarters of an inch taller and about eight pounds heavier, trifling differences compared to recent history. Jess Willard dwarfed Dempsey four years earlier, only to suffer a ferocious beating. With the exception of Jim Jeffries defeating Bob Fitzsimmons and Willard taking the title from Jack Johnson, championship belts had to be taken in to fit the smaller man in recent exchanges of that coveted accessory. Based on the published comparisons between Dempsey and Gibbons, tailoring would not be necessary if it changed ownership in Shelby.

From neck to ankle and fingertip to fingertip, the fighters' physical differences were measured in fractions of an inch. The only area where they didn't look identical on paper turned out to be nothing more than a rumor. Gibbons felt compelled to correct it for the record. Word got around that he was thirty-four years old, six years Dempsey's senior. In the search for speculative reasons Gibbons might not be able to handle the champion, six extra years on his twenty-two-and-a-half-inch thighs sounded as legitimate as any. He admitted to only twenty-nine years (thirty-two was the truth), saying any reports to the contrary referred to his brother Mike's age. An honest mistake but significant as a contrast between two fighters otherwise indistinguishable in height, weight, and other physical artillery.

Attention remained fixed on those details for the next several days. Financial news calmed down to credulous echoing of official pronouncements from fight headquarters. They said, in essence, that everything would be fine. An audit of the books that Dan Tracy ordered revealed no malfeasance, not that any had been suspected. Promotional malpractice, perhaps, but the estimable Tracy took the job to root out that threat to the success of the enterprise. General accounting for tickets already sent around the country would be completed within a few days. On Wednesday, June 20, the Shelby promoters sent word that they expected payment in full or tickets returned by the weekend. By Monday, June 25, they would have the details tallied. Already, as the *Chicago Tribune* reported (or promised like an overdue debtor to an inquiring creditor), "there was a goodly number of checks in the mail."

It would take a goodly number of legitimate ticket sales to fill the octagonal, skeletal wooden bowl just completed with room for forty thousand. Seat numbers still needed to be painted, but they would have time to dry before anybody sat down. Whether enough people would show to make the effort of numbering the benches necessary remained an open question.

To many readers of far-flung newspapers, Shelby must have seemed as remote as Mauritius, the island in the Indian Ocean where survivors of the sunken British steamship *Trevessa* made landfall on lifeboats. And the fate of the fight itself probably seemed more tenuous than the recovery of men who spent almost a month at sea without provisions. Their prognosis looked good. As for the risk of a shipwreck in Shelby, well, the fight didn't seem to be taking on water anymore, but reasonable observers wondered whether the superficial repairs could hold.

Minor nuisances became news. Mosquitoes made the papers as an itchy infestation after the rain. Panhandlers also appeared in reports as another kind of persistent pest that tourists had to wave away. Enterprising entrepreneurs arrived by the trainload, turning Shelby into the lemonade stand capital of the Northwest. "The soft drink places increase in equal ratio to the population," the *New York Times* reported. "As each train arrives a new group starts business. Shelby's Great White Way blossomed forth the other night and every one was so proud of it the City Fathers let it burn continuously for three days and nights."

One column to the left of that condescending description of

local color, the paper informed anyone interested in braving the mosquitoes and panhandlers that a special train would run from New York to Shelby. The Metropolitan Special would leave July 1, arriving the morning of the fight. Sleeping cars would provide lodging in Shelby to avoid hotel complications. With a ringside seat and a side trip to Glacier National Park included, the trip went for $325. Spare change for lemonade, largesse to the less fortunate, and calamine lotion were not included. That would have to come out of the passenger's own pocket.

So would the cost of fortunetelling from Mysterious Milli-cent—whose nominal fee must have been a bargain for any en-terprising gambler—except her "Egyptian tent show" took on a lot of water in the storm, which damaged her reputation as a soothsayer more than her portable Main Street storefront. As Richard Henry Little of the *Chicago Tribune* wondered, if Millicent could predict the winner of the fight, "why wasn't she hep to the fact that she was going to be drowned out by the rain, huh?"

Announcements from fight headquarters in Shelby, though still vague, indicated that the region would not have its couch cushions searched for loose change. Deadlines loomed for Dempsey's final payment and the completion of arena construction and railroad siding. Shelby, if not exactly on schedule, seemed to be catching up. Three extra train platforms, the de facto hotel lobbies for many visitors in Shelby, opened for business on June 22. Two miles west of the arena in Verden, another new stand awaited trains from Canada.

The increasing infrastructure had not yet attracted an influx of guests. About the only quantifiable increase in population involved the number of concessionaires. In hot dog stands per capita, Shelby must have become the nation's leader.

Richard Henry Little noted the forlorn state of affairs among street vendors. "The proprietor of a hot dog kiosk looked across the street at the sad eyed owner of a lemon pop café. . . . 'For the love of Mike come over and eat a hot dog in my joint and I'll come over to your place and order a lemon pop.'"

Down the rails in Great Falls, Jack Dempsey went through his own hurried preparations. Like the town where he would defend his title in about ten days, he did not look quite ready. Sparring partners still took a ferocious punishment, but observers who fancied themselves experts on his physique and fighting style saw a different Dempsey than they remembered from two years earlier against Georges Carpentier. His legs appeared to be the first to go. "The lower extremities have become loose and flabby where they once were muscularly hard and flexible," the *New York Times* reported, citing unnamed "critics" so as not to seem so impertinent itself as to question his heartiness for a fight. "Particularly is this true of Dempsey's thighs, where the loose flesh shakes jellylike with the impulsive step taken by the champion. Dempsey's hitting, too, is below par, in the estimation of these critics, and his defense is not what it should be."

Big Ben Wray experienced the brutal power of Dempsey's offense, which appeared to be all it could and should be. After sluggish exhibitions against George Godfrey and Billy Wells, Dempsey disposed of Wray without showing any negative effects from those flabby legs. This particular toppling, despite testing none of the champion's boxing skill, thrilled the spectators at Dempsey's training camp because Wray had so far to fall. He stood over seven feet tall, not so much a sparring partner as the attraction in a vaudeville act. Smaller trees probably were cut down for arena lumber. In less than one round, they were yelling "Timber!" for the falling Wray.

A novice determined to challenge Dempsey despite the better judgment of his manager, Tex McCarthy, Wray folded his considerable limbs between the ropes. What followed confirmed the lessons of previous heavyweight title fights when the smaller man won. Size might be an advantage in a barroom brawl but not in the ring against a superior boxer. Wray ended up unconscious with a broken jaw but managed to sputter this insight when he came to his senses: "Man, he sure can hit." About Dempsey, even the "critics" would never doubt that.

When a storm on June 21 knocked out the electricity at Dempsey's camp, he took a forced day off. The weather made it impossible to spar or even run through the deepening roadway puddles. With no lights, the indoor ring was of no use either. That left Dempsey's contingent to sit in front of a fire playing hearts while Kearns parried those "critics" with his side of the story.

"Why, Jack Dempsey is in the best shape right now that he's ever been. He is more developed, faster, hitting harder—better in every way than before any fight in his career. In short, he is a finished fighter.

"Training? He doesn't need any more boxing. I am glad that this difficult weather gives him a chance to lay off. It is ridiculous for anyone who claims to know the champion to say that he is not in wonderful shape right now."

Gibbons did not possess the champion's thunderous power, but his fitness for the fight seemed assured without his manager's protests. Kane kept him out of the ring on June 20 to prevent a fever blister on his lip from opening up with a sparring partner's blow. Ten miles of roadwork over the spongy mud and doubled calisthenics made up for the time Gibbons would have spent sparring, but Kane worried more about working him too hard than missing precious rounds. Those practice sessions might not have been entirely challenging anyway. "During the last week some of Gibbons' assistants have been doing most of their road work on the floors of the local dance halls and this morning there was no one up in time to go on the road with Gibbons." To restrict footwork to the canvas, Kane imposed a ten o'clock curfew on the camp. The rule did not need to be applied to Gibbons, never given to carousing, and monastic in training. Vanilla ice cream passed as a vice for Tom Gibbons, and he even reduced that gallon-a-day habit to a quart while preparing for a fight. "When he travels," Mike Gibbons said, "it is difficult to drag him from his hotel."

In Shelby, Gibbons stayed home most nights with his wife and three young boys in their donated home just up the hillside from the arena. They lived as if he had a workaday job in town, punching a clock instead of sparring partners. Home for dinner in the evenings, he played with the sons he called his "outfield."

All the local attention and pressure on their father did not interfere with the roughhousing rituals of summer. Young Tommy, the eldest at age six, found a sharp stick on a scavenging mission near the arena and swiped it across the cheek of his four-year-old brother, Jack, leaving a gash like Zorro's mark. Just that day, Tommy told his dad he wanted to be a toreador when he grew up, dangerous work even for a boxer's son. Tom had something more like the law or medicine in mind for the boys, who were the inspiration in his title quest.

Resting in an armchair at his home away from home, with the older boys at his feet tangled in their own ongoing bout, Gibbons cradled his one-year-old and fed him a bottle. When Helen offered to take the baby so that Tom could continue a conversation with a visiting reporter in peace, Gibbons said no. He had few opportunities to hold little Dickie, and he wanted all the time he could get. "And, anyway, this baby likes me to sing to him." The challenger for the heavyweight championship of the world hummed the lullaby "I'll Cry over You" to the baby boy in his arms.

"Just sort of practicing up on that song," Gibbons said, "because I expect to sing it over Jack Dempsey somewhere between the first and fifteenth round on July 4."

His confidence swelled as training progressed. The recent rains often forced his entourage to tack a canvas to the floor inside the Green Light western dance pavilion, where hundreds of people would squeeze in to watch him work. Dispatching his sparring partners with speed and power many observers had not expected,

Gibbons continued to sway public opinion among people who had seen both him and Dempsey train. What once appeared to be a sure thing for Dempsey now looked like at least a fair fight and maybe one that favored Gibbons after all.

"Tommy has developed a co-ordination between mind and muscle that is capable of bewildering the most skillful puncher. If he can maintain his present speed until the day of the bout Dempsey is going to be swinging at the fastest target that ever bobbed up before him."

Conditional confidence also applied to the final payment due to Kearns. As a measure of the shape the fight was in, that meant more than the strength in Dempsey's legs or the stamina Gibbons could summon. Unlike those identifiable, if speculative, factors, the financial condition did not undergo a detailed, daily public evaluation. Reports did not reflect reality. They couldn't have. The numbers just did not add up.

During a brief grace period after the collective exhale of the second payment, writers relied on Tracy's optimistic comments for coverage of the economic angle. Alongside news of Gibbons sharpening himself to such a fine point two weeks before the fight that Kane might relax the routine, the *New York Times* of June 24 reported that the final $100,000 should be in hand within days "if present plans materialize."

If present plans, as described by Tracy, had ever materialized, Shelby could have paid Kearns, plus the lumber company and all the contractors, and paved those muddy roads into town on top of it. He claimed a rate of more than one thousand tickets per day selling just in Shelby itself. Even at the cheapest level of reserved seats, at that pace local ticket sales alone would have covered the last payment in just four days. And that represented just a fraction of over $300,000 worth of tickets distributed across the country, presumed to be hot commodities again as negative speculation cooled.

To complete a detailed audit, Tracy ordered all money collected around the country sent to fight headquarters at once, along with any unsold tickets from authorized sellers across the United States and Canada. Only then would the full financial picture come into focus. As Tracy tried to cut an optimistic posture, the conspicuous absence of hard numbers kept rumors of a financial collapse simmering.

"Tracy expressed assurance that by Monday or Tuesday something like $150,000 or $160,000 will be on hand in Shelby," but on Saturday, June 23, he would not disclose a current balance in the promotional bank account. All Tracy would divulge was that "he does not anticipate any difficulty in meeting Dempsey's third payment nor in discharging any of the voluminous financial obligations entailed in promoting the bout."

Beyond the obligations to Kearns and Dempsey, the promoters submerged the fight in so much debt that Gibbons figured to get nothing. Even if the fight was flush, gate receipts would have to exceed $300,000 before he would see a cent. He would not see a cent.

That increasing inevitability did not trouble a camp intent on acquiring a gold belt more valuable to them than money. The championship would be worth plenty of money to the owner in the long run, accompanied with priceless pride. "We are glad Dempsey will get what is coming to him financially, for he certainly is going to get what is coming to him physically," Eddie Kane said. "Let Dempsey get the money, we'll take the title."

To anyone who asked, and many did as the struggling promotion became a national preoccupation, Gibbons repeated that motivating theme. "I will fight Jack Dempsey July Fourth if there is only 30 cents left for me after the champion is paid off." In fact, he increased that ante a few days later, insisting that the fight would be worth it even if he had to pay for the privilege. "I'll fight Jack Dempsey on July 4th if it costs $5,000 for the chance."

Given the financial uncertainty, the idea of Gibbons paying for the opportunity might not have seemed so far-fetched. More than just unsettling news about the fight, even the weather reports were enough to drive down attendance. Richard Henry Little described a scene that sounded more like Lake Shelby or "Venice during a tidal wave."

Shower after ironic shower fell on the region in mid-June, not a great time for the heavens to open after years of agriculture-ravaging drought. The ill-timed rain now threatened to have the same decimating effect on the struggling tourist-import industry. "It was dry up in this part of the United States once. This was an irrigation country and somewhere down in the bottom of this new formed sea of mud are buried irrigation sluices and canals. Shelby was a farming town then. Now it's a deep sea port."

Little wrote of people using the sidewalks as floatation devices and sinking in the mud on Main Street as they stood debating the particulars of the fight. Vendors likewise found themselves up to their goods and services in grimy water. "It takes a stout heart to run hot dog, red pop or restaurant tents in this wide expanse of yellow sea. Bailing out a tent gets tiresome after a while and today 'for sale' signs appeared on many a gallant café that had sprung a leak and was going down with all hands aboard."

A generally sunny disposition prevailed in both camps, although Dempsey and Gibbons approached the business of preparation in distinct ways. With only his sparring partners, among other not-quite-as-domesticated animals, to keep him company, Dempsey operated in a rugged atmosphere of men roughing it. Not that they lacked for creature comforts in their rambling stone home, but the champion's wilderness roots ran deep, and the camp along the Missouri River brought out that side of him.

Gibbons led more or less the same life he would have at home in St. Paul. Helen cooked meals and hung the laundry to dry on the line outside. Little Tommy and Jack caused enough early morning ruckus to cut into his sleep until he concocted a plan to lull them into peace and quiet. Instead of telling them to knock it off, Gibbons encouraged them, insisting they run faster and faster until the whole idea lost its appeal. "So now they don't make any more racket," Gibbons said, "and I get more sleep."

Something about Dempsey's demeanor seemed different to the famous writer Damon Runyon. There was a more serious, sedate air about him, a sense of relaxation and confidence. As much as he thought of Gibbons, Dempsey seemed as interested in the upcoming Luis Angel Firpo–Jess Willard fight—the winner would be sure to get the next crack at him. Dempsey, his psyche betraying none of his apparent physical decline, had no apprehension about who would win his bout.

The younger Dempsey had been restless and high-strung in the run-up to a bout. Now he seemed more mature, as if fame, time, and a trip abroad had mellowed him, although he still laughed like a little kid when Wild Bill Lyons lost his toupee during some impromptu roughhousing.

"He has changed a lot," Kearns said. "He has changed since the trip to Europe. I think that trip, and his contact with the people over there not only broadened him, but settled him down. He is not nearly as restless as he used to be."

Runyon had another theory. On a trip into town with Dempsey, the champion sent a long telegram to Los Angeles, "costing several dollars," addressed to a "distinctly feminine" recipient. Perhaps the male camaraderie of his training camp did not agree with him as much as it appeared.

Like something out of a script Frank Capra had not yet written, Gibbons lived in a scene of domestic bliss. When Runyon arrived at his house in Shelby, the middle child greeted him at the door.

"My name's Jack."

Runyon gestured toward the window, where Dickie clutched a spoon and gurgled from his carriage. "Who's that in the window?"

"That's Dick," Jack said. "Did you know Eddie Kane's dog bit me?"

Before the famous reporter could process that dog-bites-boy story, an older boy appeared with the uniform of a Boy Scout but an imagination for the range.

"My name's Tom. I'm a regular cowboy."

Helen Gibbons was the next to greet their guest, apologizing for her husband, who was shaving and would be out in a moment. They waited on the porch, where the Shelby of old could be seen and the new could be heard.

"We could look out over the town of Shelby, drying out in the sun," Runyon wrote. "Wagons and motor cars went grinding through the mud. From every corner of the town came the noise of hammers and saws as men worked busily on new buildings and dwellings."

It was an unusual setting in which to find a heavyweight title contender. The swelling of romantic music could almost be heard between the lines. In fact, there was the tinny sound of a mechanical piano from Shelby's entertainment district "now vastly subdued by the efforts of old John Law."

A man of simple tastes and determined focus, Gibbons just bobbed along about his business amid the background noise, cooing to his baby boy, and contemplating how he could achieve the unexpected against Dempsey. More than physical superiority would be necessary, he felt sure. Gibbons intended to seek out a psychological edge.

Throughout his career he tried to turn the meeting in the center of the ring before a fight into a staring contest. Looking an opponent in the eye, especially when it appeared to make the other man uneasy, inflamed Gibbons's confidence. "I do this with all opponents, having discovered that the effect on myself is as great as it is on them." Dempsey seemed more inclined to glance at the scene around him, which obviously did not reflect a lack of belief in himself, but Gibbons imagined the champion's averted gaze would benefit him. "Did you ever notice how superior you feel toward a man who doesn't look you in the eye?"

Dempsey, meanwhile, was preoccupied with pinochle. He considered himself the champion of that pastime too and lamented how his camp mates drifted away from the card table once he started winning. That required him to lure some newspapermen into the game, "throwing" a few hands at first so they did not recognize his expertise and run. "Well, those tricky boys must have known I was under a 'pull' and they won't play with me anymore and I'm $10 out, so what's the good of being a champion at this pinochle game anyway?"

Shelby awakened to sunshine on June 25, and the promoters treated the blue skies as a prophecy. Tracy deferred the financial report promised for that day, offering only his usual fuzzy confidence, this time using the weather forecast as a sort of meteorological collateral. Sunshine would attract the tourists who had so far stayed away, not because of the persistent uncertainty about the fight, but to avoid getting wet. Now, with the sun shining and the roads drying, they had no more impediments.

"Shelby for many years was called the town that God forgot—now it is the biggest little town in the world—and the most talked of," the *Boxing Blade* boasted. "All roads from June 25 to July 4th will lead to the town that everybody will remember."

Considering all the financial injuries the battered fight promotion suffered, it would be difficult to pinpoint the moment whiplash occurred, but forensics suggest that the biggest jolt occurred on June 26–27.

"FINANCIAL CRISIS PASSED AT SHELBY," the *New York Times* announced, reporting news of a favorable deal with the arena's lumber and construction companies. H. A. Templeton of the Monarch Lumber Company and the contractor Jack Humphreys, among several others, agreed to waive their claims, which reports estimated between $73,000 and $85,000, until gate receipts were collected. That, in effect, freed the promoters to use all available funds for the third installment to Kearns.

The deal did not come without internal tension. Several hours into the negotiation, George Stanton emerged "obviously ill-tempered" and reported a contingency plan in the event that the contractors followed through with their stated threat. He said that they intended to foreclose on the arena, and the promoters promised to seek an injunction from the state supreme court to postpone any action until after the fight. An hour later, Stanton was summoned back to the conference room, where they hammered out the agreement to pay the contractors out of the gate receipts, preventing another economic catastrophe and potential litigation.

So they had that settled, and everybody sighed with relief, until . . .

"FAILURE THREATENS DEMPSEY TITLE BOUT," the *Times* blared the next day. Ten days after he took over, Dan Tracy resigned abruptly and painted a dire picture with his parting remarks. "Tracy gave as his reason the apparent failure of the bout, the fact that the third $100,000 due Dempsey was not in sight and his disinclination to be a last-minute 'goat' in the failure of the undertaking." He offered a dollar figure this time, saying there was "less than $300 in the fight treasury."

That changed the subject.

Mayor James A. Johnson, who stood to lose the most money of any individual involved in the promotion, made swift assurances that Tracy's departure would not lead to the cancellation of the fight. Any hope for financial success had suffered a knockout blow, Johnson acknowledged, but he and other backers vowed to carry on anyway, even with no earthly clue how they might raise the final $100,000 installment. Part of Johnson's personal real estate fortune, he said, could be tapped if it came to that. Only a day earlier, official word from Shelby made the cutting of that check out of traditional promotional proceeds sound like an imminent formality.

Tracy now maintained that he had come to Shelby only to collect $17,500 on behalf of Great Falls businessmen who contributed that amount toward the second $100,000 installment. He could not recoup their investment or, for that matter, verify any sales figures or ticket availability. "I understand that $500,000 worth of tickets has been sold, but I cannot get a check on the tickets or the money. I am tired of waiting around and doing nothing."

Whether the promoters could make good on their vow to hold the fight despite the dire circumstances now depended on Kearns. They had three days to pay, or Kearns had every right to leave town with his $200,000 and Dempsey untouched. That sounded like just the kind of thing he might do.

There was pressure on Kearns to put Dempsey in the ring no matter what. The champion's popularity already suffered from his "slacker" reputation. To take $200,000 and run, leaving a new arena empty, a town bankrupt, and a challenger without a paycheck, would risk alienating a wider swath of the public. Of course, Dempsey held the title until someone took it away, so he and Kearns would not want for dance partners.

In their meetings with Kearns, the staggered, helpless Shelby promoters must have understood how Jess Willard felt under Dempsey's unrelenting assault. Kearns struck a delicate balance in public, taking a hard line on the matter of his third installment while appearing to cooperate with fight officials. The wheezing enterprise needed a simple, declarative statement from him that Dempsey would fight July 4, but he never went quite that far.

At a meeting with reporters in Shelby on June 27, Kearns said only: "I believe the fight will come off. . . . Dempsey is still training and will continue to train and I have every confidence in Mayor Johnson and the promoters of the fight to carry out their agreement with me." A politician could not have polished that stance to a higher shine.

To say with certainty that the fight would happen would have ceded leverage to the promoters. Regardless of what the contract said, they could have withheld the final installment as a political maneuver if Kearns had been more direct in his statement. Instead, he talked around the central issue in language that sounded optimistic but did not omit the importance of the last $100,000 in producing a favorable result for all parties.

Doubt reigned in Shelby. Despite Johnson's assurance that he could cover the balance of the contract, a fund-raising campaign continued, to no avail. The property that Johnson possessed might not have interested Kearns anyway, considering he turned down the offer of a three-thousand-acre Montana ranch, on the market for $150,000, in lieu of payment. The ranch known as R. A. Harlow, considered "one of the show places of central Montana," did not entice Kearns any more than the fifty thousand head of sheep.

Runyon sympathized with his plight. He outlined the conflicting tensions tugging at Kearns. If he carried on with the fight without receiving the final payment, "sportsmanship will have triumphed to a certain extent, but a precedent will have been established that will make other managers of pugilistic properties most uneasy." That is, competition would be valued above commerce, an idea "that would be intensely damaging to the managerial mob" Kearns represented as the de facto boss. Then again, Dempsey's earning power depended on his popularity, which would suffer if he walked away from a fight most observers considered an easy knockout with $210,000 in charity. "It is certainly one extremely delicate problem," Runyon said, "requiring mental operation of singular nicety and skill."

And frequent wardrobe changes. On June 29, a day of repeated run-ins with the promoters, Kearns emerged from his hotel room multiple times wearing a different suit and hat. "No one knows whether this is for sartorial effect or a disguise," Robert Edgren said. "Whichever it is, Johnson did not lose the trail once."

James A. Johnson, a hunter, could not have missed the dapper "draping of gabardine" that did not blend into the environment. Johnson did phone first, before breakfast, apparently offering some sort of "proposition." To the reporters eavesdropping outside his room, Kearns did not sound open to negotiation.

"What do you mean—proposition? I don't know anything about propositions. The contract is the only proposition I know about. The only new proposition I can hear has to have a rustle like $100,000. If that's what you mean, shoot it right along."

Sheep, shares in the oil field, a ranch, none of it moved Kearns. With Shelby offering only grass instead of cash, the opinion prevailed that he would have to take his final pound of flesh from the gate receipts. He would not commit to that. Empty hope and even a hoax kept Shelby vibrating like a tuning fork at every plot twist. Rumor after rumor surfaced that magnates from around Montana, or interested railroad and telegraph companies, would ride to the rescue, only to be denied.

A telegram dated June 28 and addressed to James A. Johnson appeared to be the collateral the fight needed:

Am leaving St. Paul to-night with sufficient cash and securities stop Assure you Gibbons friends and fight fans will not allow fight plans to fail stop Want Tom to have opportunity to put profiteering Dempsey in hospital
LOU W. TILL

The promoters believed it to be a legitimate offer, not from a "Lou W. Till," but from Louis W. Hill, the chairman of the Great Northern Railroad. It was the transparent hoax it appeared to be, but no potential gift could be dismissed without a little investigating. Like so many other moments in the fight promotion, this one could be characterized by fleeting exhilaration and eventual disappointment.

The ongoing financial mess solidified Dempsey's role as the villain in the local drama. Shelby all but adopted Gibbons as its own, and the Blackfoot tribe actually did. Gibbons and Chief Curly Bear led a parade of Blackfeet in front of the grandstand at the Shelby stampede. Indians drumming tom-toms provided the beat as the group filed into place with several thousand spectators awaiting the ceremony that would install the challenger as a member of the tribe. May Aubrey, a bareback rider and Indian princess known as "Many Victories," interpreted the chief's oration. He made an announcement to the tribe, and "they all chanted a weird song," before kneeling in front of Gibbons. Reaching toward the sky with his right hand and touching the ground with his left, Chief Curly Bear addressed the spirits on the boxer's behalf:

Oh Holy Son, I am praying to you to give strength to our son of the north so that he may be victorious in his fight. Oh holy father, our saviour, to make my son strong so that he may win his fight. Oh thunder and lightning that comes from the southwest, with your strength and swiftness, make our son just as strong and as quick as lightning and true as the stars above. All of you be with him when he fights.

This will give you sufficient strength to win.

Completing that prayer, Chief Curly Bear stood and put his hands on Gibbons's head. "The name of my son shall be Thunder Chief."

Curly Bear shook hands with Gibbons, leading a receiving line that included "all the chiefs and bucks, as well as the squaws, children and papooses." They took turns wishing him well, and Thunder Chief called them all brother or sister.

Leading citizens of Montana like James A. Johnson and George H. Stanton felt that the honor of the state was at stake. Failing to hold the fight now, whatever the cost, would be a staggering punch to the struggling state's solar plexus. Johnson already had put up more money than anyone. Stanton put $50,000 in the hat the promoters passed to collect the second installment. They could take the financial loss but not the damage to Montana's reputation if, after all this, the fight never happened.

Appealing to that sense of state loyalty, they lobbied other Montana men of means to help them see their contractual obligations through. Major Gene Lane of Lewiston and Judge Roy E. Ayers of Great Falls joined Stanton in a hotel room on June 29. This makeshift fund-raising committee sent telegrams to many of their wealthy friends around the state. Within five hours, their pledge drive received commitments from twenty people at $5,000 each, all certain enough for Stanton to pronounce their efforts a success. The money would be in the bank in twenty-four hours and presented to Kearns two days later, July 2, as specified in the contract.

Pride alone did not inspire the contributors to participate. Johnson, Molumby, and even Kearns forfeited their share of the motion picture rights to them. All the original interested parties were now removed from the promotion, and Major Lane assumed control. It was an amicable agreement, even loosening Kearns's grip on part of the enterprise. As Major Lane said: "Mr. Kearns, realizing that there had been some previous mismanagement and being desirous of helping to assist me in my endeavors, voluntarily agreed to assign all of his and all of the champion's interests in the moving picture rights, privileges and contracts as an additional bonus to those who contributed the final $100,000."

In hindsight, even that gesture turned out to be just another Doc Kearns con. He knew—and, more important, he knew the promoters did not know—that a federal law prohibited the interstate trafficking of fight films. "Such a concession was worthless," except as an act of faux good faith from Kearns to calm the financial distress. Of course, that little practical joke would not be discovered until Kearns had long since passed into Shelby infamy.

Elmer Davis of the *New York Times* arched the first eyebrow at the idea that the final $100,000 installment could, in fact, be collected as promised. Even if that amount could be raised, the number of people with a legitimate claim on a portion of it went far beyond Kearns. "A real estate title on Manhattan Island will be a simple thing to the tangle of agreements, provisos, attachments, contracts and injunctions that will have to be straightened out after the fight. Montana might find it was the easiest way out if the last $100,000 could not be raised after all."

News of the twenty IOUs from around Montana settled the question for many. Davis considered the situation "more muddled even than it had been." That was saying something, considering "a sporting writer who had been a war correspondent in France remarked . . . that next to the late war this prize fight was the muddiest and muddledest affair he had ever seen."

For the moment, euphoria over the latest promised resuscitation overshadowed all the other issues. Feeling vindicated, Mayor Johnson telephoned from Great Falls to inform the newsmen in Shelby of the deal. "You can tell the cock-eyed world that the battle will come off July Fourth with bells on." This set plans in motion for another patented Shelby celebration, "a hot welcome" for Johnson when he returned from Great Falls. "All is enthusiasm and every person here has appointed himself a committee of one to get behind Jim Johnson and make the fight a success." Musicians were summoned and cars sent to rustle up "all the Indians and cowboys" to lead a parade for Johnson when he arrived.

By now, Shelby had become a three-shift carnival, a round-the-clock carousel of activity. Buildings of plain pine had sprouted up, not the facilities for forty thousand in the original plan, but a noticeable addition to the landscape alongside existing places like the Silver Grill and the King Tut.

Temporary venues also pitched tents in town, like the one Kearns remembered featuring "a series of plays called *Which One Shall I Marry, Thorns and the Orange Blossoms, The Tie That Binds,* and *The Sweetest Girl in Dixie.*" On his business trips to Shelby, Kearns soaked up the local color. Part of him must have admired the brazen spirit on display there, even as the other, more dominant side of his brain plotted to exploit it. Naturally, Aunt Kate's Cathouse also did not escape his wandering eye.

Kearns also noticed the increase in cars and carriages parked along the plains and the extra railroad cars on the expanded siding. To him, that represented real interest in the fight, even if the crowds paled in comparison to the expectations. There was still enough traffic to get an entrepreneur to thinking. During the day, knots of people clustered on the shady side of Main Street, making it difficult to maneuver. "Mary Ellen, the horned horse, has returned to town. A 'Soak the Cullud Gent' game has been opened on Main street and, all in all, Shelby has begun, as it were, to perk up." At night, sleeping accommodations were scarce, although there was an occasional, out-of-the-way vacancy.

"Rear seat for sleeping, 50 cents," read the sign on a car parked along Main Street. The proprietor of this four-wheeled hotel was not about when a reporter passed. A friendly neighbor suggested he hop in anyway and go to sleep—"the owner would collect in the morning."

Shelby was alive with activity, but the unseen bustling at the fight offices would have revealed that all was not well. The promoters were not organizing parades or sampling the available delicacies and curiosities even after the supposed rescue of the fight and Montana's honor once and for all. They remained mired in a dire financial situation, lost amid the misleading reports and the subsequent revelry. There was nothing to celebrate because the promises that set off the latest round of carousing were not kept.

Most of the men who pledged a $5,000 contribution did not deliver. Cash transactions for tickets hardly could have covered the cost of a visit to Aunt Kate's Cathouse. It took all the rope these Montana ranchers could muster to lasso Dempsey, and the failed promotion had fashioned it into a noose.

Promoters convened with Kearns in Great Falls on July 2, prepared to topple the rickety chair beneath them and surrender. Their efforts to raise the final $100,000 had failed, and Major Lane made a statement to that effect at 2:30 in the afternoon. The committee would remain intact until midnight, as a formality, but its work ceased immediately. "The matter is now in the hands of Promoter Molumby and Jack Kearns. It is they who will decide whether there shall be a bout on Wednesday afternoon."

Before his public statement, Lane told Kearns the fight treasury showed a balance of only $10,000, which turned out to be about $6,000 too optimistic. Lane urged Kearns to put Dempsey in the ring anyway and rely on the gate receipts. Many believed that he would agree to do that but not before the midnight deadline passed without payment.

Opinions about the next move that Kearns would make swirled in the Park Hotel lobby among reporters, curious citizens, and various boxing hangers-on. Many believed that he had no choice but to deliver Dempsey to the ring. All the reasons were sound. He could not risk the damage to the champion's reputation or to the sport itself. With $200,000 already deposited, he wasn't exactly passing the hat to collect for Dempsey's next meal. His fighter, fine-tuned from six weeks of training, needed the challenge more than the money anyway. Of course, this was Doc Kearns they were talking about, the con to contradict all the pros. "Against that the other side reasoned that Mr. Kearns was never known to take less than the contract price, so why should he now?"

Elks Lodge conventioneers from around the state provided the sound track to the drama, if not quite in tune with the events or each other. Bands, plural, played in the lobby and marched through the halls of the hotel all day and through the night. "In intervals they turned the fire hose down hotel elevator shafts and committed other little pleasantries." Only at the Park Hotel, with fight news dominating everyone's attention, could a marauding band of Elks cause so much of a ruckus and attract so little notice.

If anything, that kept the guests who wanted peace and quiet from complaining about all the reporters knocking on doors to dig up the latest gossip.

Upstairs in his room, Kearns wrestled with his decision while doing some pro bono work as a trainer. A reporter from New York had fallen at dinner that night, and Kearns rubbed the liniment camphor into his weary legs. Inhaling the menthol scent and cigarette smoke, Kearns tried to make up his mind.

A few minutes after 11:00 p.m., reporters relayed a comment to Kearns from George H. Stanton that changed the tenor of the proceedings from tense to antagonistic. Stanton said legal counsel informed the promoters that failing to pay the final installment did not represent a breach of contract and that Dempsey still had an obligation to fight. Hearing that opinion "caused a visible change in his manner."

Minutes before midnight, in a room choked with smoke at the Park Hotel, Kearns wore a straw hat askew and looked askance at the latest hopeful trial balloon from the prodigal promoter, Loy J. Molumby, who wondered aloud if $25,000 might be enough to appease Kearns.

"Loy, do you think you could raise fifty thousand?" Kearns said. "I'd take the gate for the rest."

"I don't know," Molumby said. "I'll try."

"I want to know," Kearns said, frustrated from navigating so many detours to the money owed him.

Of course, Kearns did know. Everybody did. Neither Molumby nor anyone else could raise $50,000 at this point. Even Molumby's $25,000 suggestion sounded like a condemned man's final lie to elude the electric chair. More than that had come in from the businessmen's pledges, but, without the full $100,000, the promoters knew they were beaten.

A dejected Stanton explained to Kearns that less than half the pledges were fulfilled and that the promoters could not, in good conscience, use that money as superficial protection against the

inevitable. "Eight of them came through but, under the circumstances, I do not feel that I can keep their money," Stanton said.
"I guess that the fight will have to be called off."

Kearns countered again with an offer to accept $50,000 and
rely on gate receipts for the rest, but Stanton insisted that would
not be possible. No other sources of funds were available.

"All right, then, that goes for me," Kearns said. "It's off."

Frank Walker, a young lawyer from Butte, had come to Shelby
at the promoters' request to flex his legal muscle and convince
Kearns to "listen to reason." Like so many who encountered
Kearns, frustration overcame Walker's reason.

"Here in Montana," he said, according to legend and echoed
by Kearns, "we have trees on which to hang fellows like you."

Kearns walked over to the window and looked out on Shelby's
expansive, grassy landscape, where only the earth's rotation created shade. "You know, Mr. Walker," he said, "I can't see a single
tree out there."

That yarn appeared in Bill Corum's reminiscence of his Shelby
experience, a scene and dialogue described in firsthand detail.
Walker disputed the specifics but not the general tone he took
toward Kearns.

Walker had been roused from his bed in the Rainbow Hotel late
in the evening of July 2. Johnson and Lane telephoned to request
his presence at the Park Hotel. They wanted legal counsel in their
ongoing, going-nowhere discussions with Kearns. Idealist that he
was, Kearns preferred to operate man-to-man with the promoters, hoping that they could work out their differences without
lawyers entangling the details. So Walker recused himself from
the proceedings.

A little while later the group, with both sides represented, told
him their proposal for a compromise. They would postpone the
fight two weeks, figuring enough revenue could be generated in
that time to pay the bills. Speaking as a visiting spectator, not an
attorney, Walker cast an emphatic nay vote for that idea.

"I came a hundred and fifty miles from Butte to see this fight, but two weeks from now I wouldn't travel ten miles to see it," Walker said. "And if I live nearby and feel this way, what about all the people who have come by special trains and who arranged excursion trips? Do you think you'll get them back in two weeks? If you don't hold the fight on the Fourth you might as well call the whole thing off."

Kearns had good reason to be content with that outcome. He reminded everyone of his "no money, no fight" stance, all but licking his fingers to flip through the figurative $210,000 bankroll already in his possession. That grandstanding reminder of the money Montana had already spent did, in fact, start Walker's mind wandering to the potential of vigilante justice.

"I got a bit sore," he wrote in response to Corum:

I didn't make the crack about there being plenty of trees being convenient for hangings that Bill Corum attributed to me.

But I did tell Kearns that if they didn't go through with it, they'd be lucky if they did get out of Montana with the money or perhaps even without it, since there were a lot of men packing guns who were milling around who might feel mighty aggrieved if the fight didn't go off on schedule.

If not a threat of imminent hanging, Walker's warning left open the possibility that other citizens might have different negotiating tactics than the men in the room with him. That prompted Mike Trant, providing security for Kearns, to mutter something about "a punch in the nose" for Walker, who had his own backup.

A friend of Walker's barked back, "Who's going to do it to him?" and that stalemate passed without punches or even more harsh words. It appeared to be all macho posturing, with both sides settling down to discuss the thorny business at hand.

Kearns, whose broad smile conveyed his righteous sense of self—a signed contract made him all the more smug—knew he had the right to walk away. But even he could not convince himself that exercising that right was the right thing to do.

He presented his case to the assembled press, who would not take "no fight" for an answer. Runyon, Grantland Rice, and Heywood Broun, among others, applied the pressure their prominence bestowed. Either that, or they were just dizzy from twists and turns of the last twenty-four hours. "Endeavoring to keep fresh, up-to-the-minute bulletins pumping over the wires," Rice wrote, "Broun, Runyon and the rest of us had long since gone nuts."

Their sane take on the situation helped keep Kearns from skipping town and taking Dempsey with him. From them, the arguments that had been bouncing around hotel lobbies all week carried real weight. They were not mere pundits but true shapers of public opinion, and Kearns took their advice to heart.

Feeling a pang of sympathy, or something, Kearns thought of all the people already up in Shelby anticipating a spectacle. Not the crowd Shelby envisioned, to be sure, but nevertheless a hearty collection of curiosity seekers. Kearns calculated—he was always calculating—that most of them probably had not purchased tickets in advance. That meant they had not contributed to his first $200,000 take and, in that case, represented another possible revenue stream flowing in his direction. "As long as we were this close, I analyzed, we might as well collect from those who still hadn't bought tickets."

The thought of all those potential buyers finally sold Kearns. At 2:45 a.m. on July 3, less than thirty-six hours before the scheduled bell, he agreed that Dempsey would fight and accept his final installment from the gate receipts. "Or, as Kearns ironically put it," Elmer Davis wrote in the *New York Times*, "[from] the first $100,000 of the gate."

When Molumby, Lane, Ayers, and Stanton returned from their final committee meeting at the Rainbow Hotel, they conferred for a few anxious moments with Kearns. In effect, they handed all the tickets and the money in the till to him, a welcome, albeit one-sided, transfer of ownership. It assured, once and for all, that the on-again, off-again fight would occur as scheduled, if not at all as planned.

Lane let the punchy collection of newspapermen know. The details were muffled amid the applause for his first words: "Boys, the fight is on."

After the confusion settled over whether the fight would happen at all, a consensus formed on who would win. Gibbons had been impressive in training, but the sheer force of Dempsey's slugging power seduced almost every prognosticator. Most expected the champion to retain his title in a knockout within the first few rounds.

Heywood Broun did not consider himself qualified to predict. To give his readers an educated guess, he visited "Esmerelda, the gypsy fortune teller, whose booth is on Main street just beyond the tent of Mary Ellen, the horse with eight horns."

"Esmerelda," he said, "who will win the big fight on July 4?"

"Who's fighting?"

A card-carrying member of the information business, Broun told her who.

"Which one do you want to win?"

Broun said Dempsey, and Esmerelda put two fingers on top of his head and held them there.

"Dempsey," she said after a minute of channeling Broun's brain. "He will win."

"But in what round?" Broun said, ever the dogged reporter.

"What's a round?"

He suggested Esmerelda just pick a number, any number, between one and fifteen. Her crystal ball told her two.

"Our prediction," Broun reported, "is that Jack Dempsey will knock out Tommy Gibbons in the second round. . . . After all, it seems to us that Esmerelda's guess is just as good as that of any other expert."

And just about the same as everyone else's.

10. Standing Their Ground

Friction threatened to erupt into a riot outside the arena as the appointed hour arrived. A skirmish between ticket sellers and would-be buyers had become a spirited preliminary bout in itself with mob rule prevailing.

"One-Eyed" Connolly, the famous gate-crasher, was just one of many who made it into the arena for free on July 4. He entered disguised as an ice delivery man, carrying a frozen block on his shoulder. It turned out to be unnecessary camouflage. All he did was beat the rush. Connolly could have waited and broken through the fence with everyone else.

Agitation at the arena perimeter increased all afternoon with cut-rate tickets doing little to attract customers or calm the protestors. A security officer set off a rush through the fence and around the box office. "If you don't have the guts to break in," he said, "then stay out." That inspired a collective surge of intestinal fortitude.

C. A. Rasmussen, the tax collector, described waves of people that "poured in" after the barbed wire fence around the perimeter had been cut. There were men and women, including some holding babies, who ignored the warning shots sheriff's deputies fired and flooded the ramps toward the bleachers. Some women caught their dresses on the fence and pushed through anyway, perhaps figuring the cost of needle and thread would be worth the free admission.

There was room for many more. Because tickets sold accounted for only part of the attendance, estimates varied between twelve and twenty thousand people in the arena for the main event—half full at best. Still, they cheered and jeered like a much larger crowd.

The ring announcer held a cone-shaped megaphone to his mouth to introduce the competitors. He might not have needed even that little bit of amplification for the crowd gathered so close to the ring to hear him, although their vocal participation required all the volume the announcer could summon.

"Ladies and gentlemen, I take pleasure in introducing Tommy Gibbons, the contender for the title of the heavyweight championship of the world."

"I have the pleasure of introducing the Manassa Mauler, Jack Dempsey, heavyweight champion of the world."

Fans and the fighters alike were lathered and buzzing with pent-up anticipation as the ceremonial preliminaries ended with the nerve-jangling sound of the ringside bell.

Dempsey and Gibbons knotted, alternately throwing thudding body blows and clinching, introducing themselves. Interlocked with Dempsey, Gibbons felt the champion's power. "Quick, wrenching strength," Gibbons said. It took everything Gibbons had just to tie him up, but Dempsey untangled his right arm and delivered three blunt blows to the back of the head.

Out of a clinch, a sudden right to the face from Gibbons did not dull Dempsey's faculties. He responded with a right to the forehead that "felt like being slugged with a brick." When Gibbons saw the right hand start to move, he anticipated a Dempsey tactic he had studied and prepared to counter. He often feinted with his right hand to create a diversion from the incoming left. This time Dempsey led for real with his right and Gibbons felt trapped, forced to lean into it as the least damaging alternative. If he moved to his right and absorbed the blow on the jaw "maybe I'd land in the cheap seats." Jerk his head the other way, and "he'd tear half my face off." He met Dempsey's right hand halfway instead, ducking a little so it caught him high on the head, blurring the clear picture he had formed of his strategic path to the title. One vicious punch disrupted months of visualization and threatened, in the first round, his journeyman's pride in always finishing on his feet.

"Lights flashed before my eyes and the ring whirled crazily," Gibbons said. "If I'd ever been knocked off my feet before, I'd have kissed the canvas there. But I'd never learned how to fall down." Many heavyweights with otherwise sturdy legs learned how to fall down from Dempsey.

With another opponent rendered vulnerable, Dempsey presumed to complete that hard lesson again with tenderizing combinations to the body. Gibbons covered up, using the ropes for support, until he stabilized himself after the punch that must have surprised him as much as it hurt. It went against his meticulous deconstruction of Dempsey's methods. He didn't abandon the plan to box, but now Gibbons had no choice but to fight.

Bracing himself against the dull ache of repeated blows to the ribs, he blocked punches with his forearms and hugged Dempsey for dear life. Between the heavy bag treatment from the champion, Gibbons inserted a left and a right to either side of Dempsey's head. He responded in kind with a punch sharp enough to cut

Gibbons. Salty blood dripped into his mouth, and Gibbons held Dempsey as the bell ended the first round.

"Eddie Kane was plenty worried," Gibbons said. "As I sat in my corner I gave thanks for that six miles of daily roadwork I'd done along the prairie ridges near Shelby. . . . My legs felt strong and loose."

His mind was still foggy from that one punishing punch, but he felt confident in his conditioning and the transformation of long hours of instruction into instinct. Until the mental blur cleared, he could feel his way. But he had to buy time. Gibbons tucked himself headfirst into Dempsey like a long-lost friend hugging him around the midsection. Clinch. Dempsey threw him off, shoving him toward the ropes, and Gibbons danced out of range. They spent most of the second round in that awkward waltz, Gibbons venturing in with a few exploratory licks and then clamping his arms around Dempsey like a combination lock. Clinch.

This had the same effect on Dempsey as waving a red cape in front of a bull. In his snorting frustration, however, he lost some control over his punches. After four, five, six swings and misses, Gibbons lassoed him again, and Dempsey drove more short-range slugs to the body and the back of the head. One wild punch caught Gibbons below the belt, aggravating the hernia that nagged him for much of his career. It aggravated the crowd too, already hostile to the champion, and now roused to howl in empathy with Gibbons. They knew how he felt.

Much to his good fortune, Montana boxing rules did not prohibit clinching as a defense. So Gibbons continued to turn the fight into a halting exhibition of fits and starts to neutralize Dempsey's coiled power and stabilize his own physical and mental moorings. That left Dougherty to pry the fighters apart as best he could without the threat of disqualifying Gibbons, and the referee "sweated gallons at the work."

After one forced separation in the second round, Gibbons felt sufficiently rejuvenated to land a left hook that opened a cut above Dempsey's eyebrow. At the sight of the champion's blood, the crowd again formed a lustful chorus cheering for his defeat, smelling it now. Gibbons had drawn blood, but the cut was a remnant from training camp. It didn't need much force to rupture. The blow hadn't done the damage that the bloody result indicated.

Both boxers continued on their collision-and-clinch course. Dempsey stalked, preying like the panther of so many newspaper similes. Gibbons stalled, praying to stay out of the way of the mauling that made those similes apt. When the bell rang, they were knotted again, physically at least, if not on the cards of the judges, who had scored the first two rounds for Dempsey.

Rising for the third round, Gibbons felt like himself again, strong, clearheaded, crisp in his timing. He did not retreat or try to wrap up Dempsey as often. Gibbons fought him off with punches at once defensive and aggressive. Dempsey crowded him to apply more of those short-range, spring-loaded combinations to the body. He had to hit a moving target behind a hail of sharp, protective punches. "I kept on the move," Gibbons said, "and forced him to wade through a cross-fire of jabs, hooks and right crosses."

Enough landed to limit the damage from Dempsey's invasion, if not to hurt the champion. He exposed himself to quick flurries like the left jab–right cross combination he absorbed because Gibbons didn't have the power to knock him down. So Dempsey accepted a few punches in exchange for working the body from the proximity that made all of his blows a threat to knock the breath out of Gibbons for good. Dempsey had the power that Gibbons did not, but, while his body work made dents, he couldn't land the shattering haymaker. "A wicked right uppercut" whiffed in the third round, and the close encounter continued. Like two soldiers wielding bayonets, they approached and parried, conservative because every brash move carried risks for both of them.

Each attempt Dempsey made for a decisive punch either missed or glanced just enough to leave Gibbons upright.

As the third round wound down, the most active three minutes of the fight so far crested like a wave. A hard right from Dempsey landed high on Gibbons's left side. That one did knock the wind out of him. Gibbons felt like the punch had cracked a rib and hunched over in labored breathing agony, gulping at the hot Shelby air in a panic. Dempsey staggered his weakened challenger with series of hooks to the head before Gibbons could back away and create a little room to breathe. His personal space disappeared in an instant as Dempsey sensed his opportunity and converged.

Once again choosing fight over flight, Gibbons tried to protect himself with a left hook. It caught Dempsey on the jaw and off guard, allowing Gibbons to land a right that stalled the onslaught against him. Suddenly, he seemed to be dictating, responding to Dempsey's best display of power with resilience that appeared to be his greatest source of strength. Each time Dempsey had tested him, Gibbons tapped into that and fought back.

For all the inspiration it sent coursing through his own corner and into the crowd, Gibbons acted out of desperation, and that could not fill his lungs. "The crowd, thinking I was going after the champ in earnest, went wild," Gibbons said. "But it was more of a counter attack. That body blow hurt like the blazes. I went after him to keep him from getting another shot at the same spot."

To his supporters, increasing in number with each cut-rate ticket sold and every gate-crashing offensive, it looked like Dempsey made him mad. In fact, the effect of the punch that triggered all the action lingered beyond the bell. Swept up in the emotion, an animated Eddie Kane greeted Gibbons to the corner with a pep talk.

"You had an edge there," he said. "Keep boxing. That's the stuff."

The sight of Gibbons wincing from the pain of trying to take deep breaths through battered ribs changed Kane's tone from rah-rah to recovery. Sensing the damage he had done, Dempsey emerged for the fourth round with "a savage gleam in his eyes." The infighting continued, but this time Dempsey initiated the intimacy.

"Gibbons was on the defensive and Dempsey kept crowding him." Dempsey held Gibbons with one arm and battered the challenger's body with the other. Other than connecting with a couple of rights to the face, Gibbons played the role of punching bag, or something even less threatening, for most of the round. "In a clinch Dempsey handled Gibbons like a baby." A hard punch to the heart and another in the ribs created the impression of the champion charging toward a knockout. Gibbons showed that he had enough guile left to avoid that and the strength to deliver a combination to the head that drew more blood from the cut over Dempsey's eye.

"Ride him, Tommy!" a cowboy shouted from ringside.

"Yeppee!" came a concurring opinion. "Give him the spurs!"

Despite absorbing a hook to the jaw at the bell, Gibbons returned to his corner showing signs of rejuvenation. A misstep allowed Dempsey to force Gibbons into a corner, the last place he wanted to be against the "merciless" champion. Staying clear of those danger zones had been a point of emphasis for Gibbons, who knew the damage Dempsey could inflict on a vulnerable opponent with no escape path. Finding a path through the blur of blows obstructing it gave Gibbons the same sensation the crowd felt in the third round when he roused himself from that punishment. "When I fought my way out and made him back away," Gibbons said, "it gave me a great thrill."

Dempsey's demeanor indicated something more like frustration. He had the clear advantage through four rounds, but his failure to put Gibbons on the canvas did not sit well. Years later, Dempsey admitted that he expected an easy fight, only to discover "one of the best defensive fighters I had met" standing toe-to-toe with him.

Early in the fifth round, Gibbons went on a brief offensive. He connected on two swift left jabs that jolted Dempsey, whose head jerked backward from the force. That served only to awaken Dempsey's temper, putting Gibbons back in a defensive posture. Dempsey "chased Tom about," but the challenger's famous footwork neutralized the blows he did endure. A hard punch to Dempsey's face concluded the best round yet for Gibbons and left the champion with blood and concern on his face.

"He's getting tired," Eddie Kane said in the corner, confirming what Gibbons sensed in Dempsey's eyes and increasingly flat feet. With Dempsey slumped against the ropes in his corner, his body language echoed Kane's statement. Doc Kearns appeared somewhat more energetic but hardly a picture of confidence, "talking a blue streak in his ear."

Gibbons began to weaken again in the sixth after suffering an off-balance bludgeoning that he invited with his escape of a potential knockout punch. Swinging for the win, Dempsey aimed a right hand at the jaw with even more ferocity than usual. Leaning back to elude it, Gibbons stumbled backward, as if the wake Dempsey created carried as much power as the punch itself. His head slipped through the ropes, and the champion sensed victory, delivering a left to the face and a right to the ribs of the supine, vulnerable contender. To Gibbons, "it showed [Dempsey] was very unsportsmanlike," but it did not affect his equilibrium, only his temper.

Through black-and-blue lips, Gibbons protested to Dougherty that Dempsey had thrown illegal punches with his head outside the ring. Thousands of Gibbons partisans repeated that opinion in stereo, howling at the perceived unethical conduct of the champion.

Gibbons regained his composure and returned to the business at hand. Dempsey descended again, delivering a combination that

Gibbons blocked, connecting with a right to the mouth in return. Maneuvering inside, Dempsey took to treating Gibbons like a heavy bag again, throwing punches in short, furious thrusts into his torso and midsection. Right, left, right, left. "His old shift," as Gibbons described it.

This is where his boxing education rewarded him. Even in the midst of a Dempsey offensive, Gibbons knew how to respond, an instinct by now that grew out of the boxing equivalent of book learning combined with old-fashioned conditioning. Stamina kept him standing. Study taught him how to block Dempsey's left to the body and respond "with a peach of a left hook" at the bell to end the sixth round. Dempsey's flickering eyes reflected the force of the blow, and Gibbons, feeling refreshed, smiled as he headed to his corner.

The crowd at the corner of Broadway and Seventh Avenue in New York, following the bulletins about the fight posted in the windows of the Times Building, rivaled the attendance in the Shelby arena itself. Only about one hundred showed up for the scheduled opening bell, but every blow Gibbons landed and every round he lasted attracted more curiosity seekers pulling for the challenger. They even endured rain showers just to follow the updates and add their voices, from two thousand miles away, to the chorus of cheers for an upset.

Kearns, the leader of the choir in Dempsey's corner, sensed that an upset could happen. His solo serenade of the champion after the sixth round was not a love song. He was in Dempsey's ear but did not appear to be whispering sweet nothings. Gibbons knew what Kearns was telling him over there.

"Pull up your socks, Jack, and smack the bum."

Call it a manager's motivation or just the emotion of the moment, but Dempsey danced out of his corner for the seventh round looking even more refreshed than Gibbons felt when the previous round ended. Gibbons diagnosed it as Dempsey's second wind but dismissed its potential for destructive force. "One minute you think you can't possibly go on; the next instant something clicks and you're piling in like a house afire," he said. "The champion was stronger, fresher, faster than at any time since the second."

The patient challenger endured more of Dempsey's short-range slugging with the confidence that it would deplete his energy. Not that Gibbons stood still and took it. He circled, ducked, and danced, but Dempsey's speed complicated the intricate choreography Gibbons had in mind. Coupled with the brute power that Dempsey could summon, that quickness made him a devastating force of nature. He brought both attributes to bear on Gibbons in the seventh round. His speed prevented Gibbons from maintaining a safe distance, which allowed him to unleash a punch that landed like an anvil.

Twisting to escape a punch, Gibbons left his back vulnerable, and Dempsey descended. A kidney punch "drove every bit of breath from my body," Gibbons said, although it did not look as crushing as it felt. Only he knew the true impact of the blow. In the middle of the ring, Gibbons bent at the waist and tried to buy time until he could breathe again, "pounding my side with my glove to drive the wind back."

Gibbons hid his precarious state of mind and body well. Even Dempsey did not realize it. The champion drove another punch to the same spot when, Gibbons believed, "any kind of tap on the chin" would have knocked him out. As Dempsey threw another punch, Gibbons treated it like a fastball and played catcher, gripping his arm until the referee wedged himself between them. Dempsey won the round, but the extent of damage that he had inflicted on a desperate Gibbons escaped notice.

"He appeared to be weakening under Dempsey's savage body attack," the *Great Falls Tribune* noted. That was an understatement. Gibbons described the ferocious blow as "the most agonizing moment I have ever experienced in the ring."

When he slumped onto his stool, grateful to rest his wobbly legs, "wondering if I'd ever be able to stand again," Gibbons realized how well he had held up under the circumstances. The buzz at ringside encouraged him. People were excited about the challenger holding his own and perhaps even outperforming the heavyweight champion. Gamblers with money on the favorite to win by knockout were among the few urging Dempsey to finish off the resilient challenger.

Eddie Kane and Bud Gorman were in revival mode, patching a cut on Gibbons's face, and trying to massage a little life back into his muscles. They knew that, the crowd's perception notwithstanding, Gibbons would be walking a tightrope into the eighth round.

"Take it easy, Tom," Kane said.

Like Dempsey in the previous round, Gibbons awakened with the bell, his mind clear and his legs light as he bounced on the balls of his feet into the scrum. Dempsey did more damage in the clinches, but Gibbons drove him back with a left hook. A swift jab to the face from Dempsey landed hard and "staggered Gibbons," who managed to respond with one of his own and a combination of hooks in a clinch. It became a punch-and-hug round as the fighters traded attempts and tangled, traded attempts and tangled.

This had been their clumsy ballet for much of the fight, as if some sort of magnetic attraction pulled them together when they got within arm's length. Daugherty, the straining referee, would then shove them beyond the reach of this invisible force field, and the process would repeat itself.

Early in the ninth round, Gibbons managed to keep his distance. He backed away from a sudden rush from Dempsey, but, when they clinched again, the jolting blows to the back of the head stung. A moment later, he felt something much worse. Dempsey missed low on a left hook to the torso. It landed on the groin instead.

"For God's sake, Jack, keep 'em up!" Gibbons said through the shooting pain. The accidental low blow made him nauseous for the rest of the round and his left leg numb for the duration of the fight.

More jeering toward Dempsey followed this and other blows perceived to be low. The crowd needed only the slightest provocation to release its pent-up rage at the champion. Hugh Fullerton of the *Chicago Tribune* noted that some of the ire about punches below the belt was misplaced. Blocking techniques that Gibbons employed to reduce the force of those sharp, short punches in the clinches pushed them down into that dangerous territory. He also wore his trunks high, creating an illusion of low blows that, in reality, were not. "But the fact remains that Dempsey landed low several times, fortunately without hurting the challenger or there would have been a riot."

At least Gibbons did not let on how much the blow hurt him. The effects were evident, to him anyway, in the tenth round. Gibbons tried to keep Dempsey a safe distance away with flicking lefts and rights, but, as he remembered, "I was weak and the blows had no snap." That allowed Dempsey to operate at short range with little risk of retaliation for the offensive. Two lefts to the jaw sent Gibbons backward, and Dempsey continued to advance on him. More punishment pushed Gibbons into the ropes, where the lack of accuracy cost Dempsey again.

A left hook with devastating potential missed its target, but Dempsey followed with a right to the body, and Gibbons tried to wrap up his arms. Shaking off the cobwebs, the challenger forced Dempsey backward into the ropes with a left hook that missed but foreshadowed a momentum swing in the eleventh round.

Fatigue started to weigh down Gibbons, but he believed that he had the lead through ten rounds—most objective observers would have disputed that—and summoned some more energy for the eleventh. A "drawn and tired looking" Dempsey shuffled into the center of the ring. They traded some blows, but Gibbons ducked a few, even escaping a dangerous corner and running away in a move that looked better suited to vaudeville than a prize fight. "The crowd roared with laughter," Gibbons said, "and Jack scowled."

Then Gibbons fired the last bullets in his chamber. Three rat-tat-tat lefts snapped Dempsey's head back, but the wounds inflicted were superficial at best. Gibbons absorbed more punishment around his midsection as the round ended, draining his reserve and reviving the predator in Dempsey.

In the corner between rounds, Dempsey heard more preaching and prodding from Kearns, who probably pointed out an important, impending benchmark in Dempsey's championship defense. Only Bill Brennan had lasted into the twelfth round against Dempsey, and he did not make it to the thirteenth. If Dempsey could not end it here, Gibbons would earn the distinction as the contender who stood up the longest against him.

Whether the crowd realized that or not, it put all its boisterous noise behind Gibbons as the round started. He would need all the support he could get. Swinging his way into the twelfth, Dempsey went prowling for a knockout against his weakened opponent. In that state, Gibbons felt the full, jarring force of every punch and strained to stop the bull rushing he had eluded with his defensive dance steps all day. "In the clinches he mauled me, jolting me with clubbing rights to the head," Gibbons said. "I was very tired and his rushes were getting harder to stop."

Holding became his desperate defense. At times it seemed as if Dempsey had him surrounded. Without a snap in his punches or the bounce in his legs, all Gibbons could do was hang on for dear life. As the champion invaded his personal space, Gibbons treated him like a drunk treats a lamppost. "Dempsey had Gibbons completely at his mercy in the clinches," the *New York Times* reported. "Gibbons was all at sea."

After twelve rounds of hugging and slugging, Dempsey could not have felt much better. Even with Gibbons so wobbly, he could not knock him down. The short-range blasts around the abdomen and rib cage remained a shock to the system, but they lacked the whisper of extra tailwind it would have taken to end the fight right there. When the bell rang, Gibbons became the champion's longest-standing challenger.

It felt like a thorny crown, not a laurel, but Gibbons understood its significance. Three more rounds separated him from the satisfaction of going the distance. Winning was a hollow hope by then, but he had a sportsman's sense of pride and honor in fighting the good fight. Whether he had the legs to remain standing was another matter.

A dozen rounds had taken enough out of Dempsey to give the weary Gibbons a reasonable chance to reach the final bell. They sparred, with Gibbons still able to elude a few of Dempsey's punches. In a clinch "Dempsey almost wrestled Gibbons off his feet" and threw thudding lefts to the head while his right arm had the challenger wrapped around it. As the referee separated them, Dempsey landed a blow through Dougherty's arms that landed flush on the lips, nothing like any kiss Gibbons had ever had.

By that time, however, Dempsey had just enough power left to produce a swollen lip—little more than a mosquito bite by his brutal standards. It "hurt like blazes" but not enough to knock Gibbons horizontal. Try as they might to fight through increasing fatigue, the result looked like they were under water. "Once I pushed a right to his face and we stood there and feinted while the crowd laughed," Gibbons said. "We both were too tired to move."

Early in the fourteenth round, Gibbons began to wonder whether he was too tired to stand. Then he saw the exhaustion in Dempsey's eyes and wondered whether he had one final championship punch in him. The stinging heat on his back and the searing pain in his lungs snuffed out that flicker of inspiration. All at once the oppressive elements, the physical effects of the fight, the psychological throb of certain defeat, landed on him with greater force than anything in Dempsey's arsenal. "I was awfully tired. I felt disappointed, too," Gibbons said. "I felt I had the title in my grasp in those middle rounds. But I determined to stay on my feet at all cost, to fight on to the end."

Cheers erupted and seat cushions flew as the fighters stepped toward the center of the ring for the fifteenth and final round. Only Gibbons's instinct for self-preservation exceeded Dempsey's determination for a knockout. After staggering from the force of ferocious blows, Gibbons clinched with all the strength he could muster, using Dempsey for support and forcing Dougherty to pry them apart. "As soon as they were separated, Dempsey would resume his vicious attack," the *Boxing Blade* reported. "He was after Gibbons with bulldog tenacity in his efforts to score a knockout."

They roared for Gibbons. Not for him to win. He couldn't do that at this late stage, not without the knockout punch he could not deliver even in the first few, fresh rounds. They roared for Gibbons to finish standing, to lose with dignity, to make Dempsey work to retain his belt and earn his money. It was the most the challenger—and the citizens of Shelby—could hope for now.

"The last few seconds seemed like hours to persons hoping to see Tommy stay the limit," the *Boxing Blade* reported. To Gibbons most of all. His sharp sense of the surrounding scene and the heartening comments from ringside had dulled into a hazy soup of heat, pain, white noise, and frozen time. "That fourteenth round seemed like an endless nightmare," Gibbons said, "but the fifteenth was worse."

Avoiding a knockout, finishing on his feet, became his only focus. A scowl cut through the fatigue on Dempsey's face, indicating that the champion meant what he wrote in the *Minneapolis Tribune*. Winning a decision meant little. Only a knockout would satisfy him.

Even that would not appease the critics, who now had more ammunition to support their perception of his diminishing abilities. Putting Gibbons on the canvas would make at least a symbolic statement, if not a convincing one after fourteen rounds of trying and failing. Kearns understood the value of symbolism in public opinion—besides, it might affect the next payday—so he had his head between the ropes, flapping his arms and his gums to prod Dempsey.

A man of immense competitive hunger, Dempsey probably did not need the motivation. Beyond his own corner, support from the crowd favored Gibbons with such gale force that it could not help but keep him upright. With nothing like that on his side, Dempsey had only the power of his punches to sustain him.

Impatient and worn out, Dempsey threw wild haymakers that often missed. A sharper Gibbons could have taken advantage of the openings Dempsey left with his spraying hail of punches, but he could only hold on for dear life or run for it. "Gibbons persisted in clinching and when free ran away from the champion."

Dempsey was running out of time to land the knockout blow, while Gibbons felt like the fight would never end. A crush of people pushed toward the ring, their cheers reaching a crescendo for the challenger to withstand the final barrage. "Dimly I sensed the crowd was pulling for me to give it to him, to finish on my feet," Gibbons said. "We seemed to be in one tiny, white-hot spot with a continuous wave of sound beating at us."

The sound of the crowd pressing closer, of their handlers shouting encouragement from the corners, of the final exhalations of two spent competitors. Gibbons would not go down, but he could not defeat Dempsey either. After the final bell, they lingered in a limp clinch, slumped against each other as a chaotic scene erupted around them.

"When the gong finally sounded a great cheer broke forth." Many fans poured through the ropes, and others cluttered the ring with seat cushions and sundry items they considered better projectiles than souvenirs. Daugherty, the referee, held up Dempsey's arm as the winner, the inevitable and indisputable decision, but both fighters received praise from the onrushing crowd. Their reactions to the outcome revealed that the final result did not really tell the story. Dempsey had disappointment in his eyes when Dougherty raised his hand, although anxiety about the crowd's intentions might have been another reason for the solemn expression. A smile crossed Gibbons's face, no doubt a reflection of satisfaction peeking through the frustration of defeat. Much like Shelby itself, he stood up to Dempsey until the final bell, no small challenge considering how many times his quest might have toppled.

The crowd made the connection between Shelby and Gibbons, adopting him as the champion of their cause, if not the heavyweight division. His exit "seemed more of a triumphal procession than a march homeward to tell the wife and children he had lost—and lost without receiving a cent for his work."

Gibbons provided the crowd with a modicum of pride, standing up to the champion like no other boxer ever had, a proxy for the preposterous dreams that this spectacle represented. No heavyweight title fight had gone the distance since the twenty-five-round marathon between Jim Jeffries and Tom Sharkey on November 3, 1899. Now Gibbons, Shelby's stunt double, stood up for the town to the final bell.

Even far beyond Shelby's battered and embarrassed borders, Gibbons emerged as the clear winner in public esteem. "SAVAGE BATTLE PROVES VALOR OF CHALLENGER," the *Chicago Tribune* said. "Loser Hero in Rare Prize Ring Upset."

It was not just underdog identification that made Gibbons so popular. He proved himself to be "one of the most magnificent boxers in the ring," a defensive magician with a chin chiseled out of something stronger than bone.

"Gibbons stopped punches today that would have killed an ordinary man. Persons sitting at ringside winced as Dempsey's heavy fists crashed against the St. Paul boy's body and face," the *Boxing Blade* reported. "It seemed unbelievable that a human could stand up under such a savage attack. Although he was weak and wobbly at the finish, Gibbons did not show many visible marks of the punishment he underwent, other than that his lips were cut and there were red welts over his left kidney and under his heart, where he stopped some of his powerful opponent's heavy clouts."

He felt the effects on his head, the swelling evident almost immediately. As the excitable crowd spilled into the ring to congratulate him, one fan missed with a congratulatory slap on the shoulder and caught Gibbons in the back of his head. "I winced in pain," he said. "I couldn't wear a hat for days on account of the bumps back there."

His expression reflected more happiness than pain or disappointment. While his corner men untied and tugged off his gloves, Gibbons basked in the appreciation of an adoring crowd and even received a couple of "official" visitors. Chief Curly Bear of the Blackfoot tribe made it through the throng in the ring to Gibbons's side. "Resplendent in feathers and rainbow hues," Curly Bear removed his ceremonial headdress and placed it on Thunder Chief's sweaty head.

Next came the wife of Mayor James A. Johnson, who did not stand on ceremony. She greeted the perspiring, bare-chested champion who smelled like who knows what with a hug in gratitude for his effort.

Indians danced at ringside. Cowboys howled and hurled their hats. A couple of them tried to crowd Gibbons, but Bud Gorman held them back. Another man knocked over a water bucket in the commotion, soaking the ring. The scene seemed like a celebration for the loser, the one man to whom Shelby truly felt indebted.

Gibbons did not idle among his idolators. Though they were friendly to him, if a little rough, he hustled through the crush of people as fast as he could and left the arena for his training camp, thinking only of getting home after a hard day's work. "Tell Mrs. Gibbons," he said to a friend once he arrived at the camp. Unless she picked up a copy of the extra edition the *Shelby Promoter* published moments after the fight, she would have been among the few in town who did not know the outcome.

Soon enough, Gibbons could tell his wife himself. A car ferried him up the hill to their house, where she waited inside while the two older boys lit firecrackers on the lawn. From the porch, she could have heard the crowd but not seen the action. Word of the outcome had reached her by the time Gibbons "dashed up the steps." She threw open the door and greeted him with a hug and a kiss.

"While feathered Indians, kilted Scots, cowboys and the sports of America cheered his defeated foe," Dempsey left the arena to somewhat less fanfare. It was more of a getaway. Within an hour, he was aboard his private train car bound for Great Falls.

Much like the fans and the boxing literati, Dempsey came away impressed with Gibbons. The champion was gracious in victory. "I know I hit him often enough and hard enough to drop any ordinary heavyweight," Dempsey said, "but I guess everybody is convinced now that Gibbons is not an ordinary heavyweight. . . . Nailing him was like trying to thread a needle in a high wind."

By the time Dempsey boarded a train in Great Falls the next day headed for Salt Lake City, his face showed the effects of fighting no ordinary heavyweight. Both his eyes were bruised, and nobody among the small farewell contingent was in the mood to offer raw steaks or commiserate. Hailed as a hero when he arrived more than six weeks earlier, Dempsey rode out of Great Falls more or less on a rail. The few who turned out to see him off were there to express their happiness to see him go.

"Don't hurry back!"

"I won't, boys."

Kearns had even more reason to be anxious about exiting Shelby, but he had business to transact before departing. Ticket revenue from the day's sales, such as they were, belonged to him. Concern for his personal safety was no reason not to collect. Body

Johnson recalled Kearns leaving the fight office with a black bag containing $54,000 and Rasmussen the tax man in tow.

Johnson said the government got none, owing once again to Kearns and his molasses grip. He "had prevailed upon the revenue people to give him the money because of his priority agreement with the promoters."

Rasmussen said otherwise the day after the fight, describing the amicable collection of more than $22,000 in tax revenue. "Jack Kearns, Dempsey's manager, gave every possible assistance to me," he said, "and my dealings with Kearns were very pleasant." That made Rasmussen about the only man in Montana who could say that.

Box office sales on fight day were estimated to be about $80,000. If the government got about $22,000 of that, Kearns would have been left with somewhere in the neighborhood of the $54,000 Johnson figured he hauled in his luggage.

Most of the hired muscle left with Dempsey. Only Dan McKetrick remained to provide security for Kearns and the cash. They made it to the train station, where a caboose awaited, hitched to a locomotive. Kearns arranged his transportation "with the help of the federal men."

From the caboose, Kearns noticed a man in the street strumming a ukulele. It was Hype Igoe, a famous New York boxing writer who had a few drinks after filing his story and took to serenading himself.

"This is the New York Special, Hype," Kearns said, inviting him aboard.

Igoe took him up on it, adding live music to the services available on the Kearns Caboose.

After arriving in Great Falls, the man carrying tens of thousands in cash spent the night in the basement of a barbershop, the better to avoid unwanted attention. In the morning, he peeled off $500 for a private coach to take him to Salt Lake City, where he would rendezvous with Dempsey.

Most of the tourists were not far behind Kearns and Dempsey in their own haste to get out of town, not fearing for their safety, just certain that they had experienced all Shelby had to offer. Nobody fled faster than the pilots flying the fight films to New York.

Jack Skees had the harrowing assignment of speeding reels of film on his Harley Davidson motorcycle from the arena to waiting planes. A police officer stood watch on his Harley as Skees, brandishing his badge from the National Editorial Association, waited inside the arena for the reels of film. When he received them, he would race to his motorcycle and speed toward winged delivery vehicles. This was a race, with no time to spare in delivering, developing and screening the film of the heavyweight championship fight. As Skees approached at full speed on his motorcycle, the pilots started preparing for takeoff.

"The minute that son-of-a-gun would see me coming, he'd start revving up and there'd be nothing but dust. I'd have to get in between the tail assembly and the wing, you see, and throw them in the back seat. Jesus, it was hairy as hell. I didn't know whether I was in the motor or where I was."

He emerged unscathed each time, and the planes ascended into the distance carrying the coveted footage of the fight. W. L. Smith brought the first plane into the Mineola, New York, airfield July 6 at 7:26 a.m. local time, forty-three hours after it departed Shelby. Smith took the controls in Chicago, after Dallas M. Smith flew the plane from Shelby.

Another plane landed in the same field several hours later carrying films purported to be taken with hidden cameras. A newsreel company planned a midnight showing on a Broadway roof garden of fight footage that "cameramen" gathered disguised as peanut vendors. "Small cameras were concealed in their baskets of peanuts." Those films passed federal inspection at the airfield because they did not show any fighting action.

People without planes to propel them up and out of Shelby had a harder time getting away. Train passengers filled the platforms, but, with so many cars positioned on the extra siding, they struggled to find the proper locomotive scattered among the look-alikes. Carrying suitcases and other items for the trip home, people just wandered around the rail yard trying to find the train bound for their destination.

Others inched their way in "automobiles, wagons, buggies," clogging the roadways in their haste. "Every species of automotive vehicle attempted to be among the first to get out of town." They formed a slow but orderly procession, "chugging along in gaseous formation."

Rush hour began at the final bell and lasted all night, a scene of transportation constipation that made the town's dream of a much bigger event seem misguided indeed. It would take another day or two for all the tourists to evacuate, but Shelby's leaders had good reason to feel very much alone already. They were on the hook for the most substantial losses in the fight promotion, an affair that had the opposite of its intended effect. On the most basic level, they received publicity beyond their wildest dreams and, against all odds and common sense, staged the fight after all.

Of course, the publicity could not have been worse, and the fight left the town fathers of Shelby poorer in revenue and reputation. Like Gibbons, all they had to show for their effort was the pride in being ambulatory at the end. Mayor Johnson, leaning against a doorway downtown, tried to look at it that way, offering a wry nod to his own financial condition.

"Well, we saw a fight didn't we?" Johnson said. "Slip me the price of a shave."

11. A Cut of Heaven's Gate

Shelby started to look like its old self again by the rainy morning of July 6. Benjamin's general store sold kerosene and apricots and shoelaces and calico and potatoes. Locals went into Larson's to shop for new shoes. Protected from the rain under an awning on Main Street, a couple of cowboys spit tobacco juice and made small talk about the weather. Jim Alsop, the city marshal, no longer on twenty-four-hour alert with the town now all but empty of tourists, pondered the geopolitical ramifications of President Warren G. Harding's wedding anniversary trip to Alaska. (Harding did not take Shelby up on its invitation to attend the fight while on his western sojourn.) With Harding away from Washington, Alsop noted, there was "nobody down there in the White House but that little Cal Coolidge."

Nobody, not even a functionary of the vice president's insignificance, was left in Shelby. Main Street looked unfamiliar to

Richard Henry Little in that deserted state. "Not one human soul was drinking red pop or eating a hot dog." No visitors, no vendors.

With the exception of the arena, a looming pine reminder, little evidence remained of the fight that put Shelby into hock. A banner stretching across Main Street advertising "Shelby, the Oil City" lost some of its impact when the rain made the painted letters bleed together.

The silence of the wide open spaces settled over the town again. It was quiet enough to hear the sound of numbers crunching. "If you listened you would hear a peculiar, rasping sound . . . pencils writing figures on paper and adding them up and then subtracting and dividing and finding what the total loss was."

In a letter to the local American Legion Boxing Club, James A. Johnson did the math and arrived at a net loss of $164,500. His ledger laid out what amounted to a modest set of expenses. It did not attach a value to the untenable economic combination of a botched promotion and a manipulative manager, but the bottom line provided a reasonable estimate:

Receipts

Gate Receipts:	$202,000.00
Net Loss:	$164,500.00
Total:	$366,500.00

Expenses

Paid Jack Dempsey:	$255,000.00
Paid Tommy Gibbons:	7,500.00
Paid Jack Sayles:	75.00
Paid Jack McDonald:	125.00
Paid Harry Drake:	800.00
Paid Bud Gorman:	1,000.00
Cost of Arena:	82,000.00
Less Estimated Salvage:	8,000.00 (74,000.00)
Referee:	5,000.00

Cost of Signing Bout
Expenses—Publicity and Advertising—Office,
Printing, and other misc. expenses $23,000.00

$366.500.00

"With the possible exception of a very small amount of loss
that was incurred on the part of a few subscribers to advance
tickets who did not sell them all before the day of the fight, all of
this loss was stood by 'James A.' and the James A. Johnson and
Company," Body Johnson said. "No banks participated in this
loss. No banking organization had anything to do with the loss
and no Legion organization lost any money on the fight."

That did not include losses that the local Chamber of Commerce and concessionaires reported. A tourist camp established
just to accommodate fight fans "was a fizzle," and two rodeo
companies lost a combined $55,000. The smaller-than-expected
and late-arriving crowd left the makeshift concessions at a loss.
Established hotels and restaurants managed to break even, or better, with just a couple of days of heavy traffic. Stores that stocked
up anticipating a crush of people shopping for an extended stay
found themselves with shelves full of unsold merchandise.

Within a week of the fight, both Stanton Trust and Savings
in Great Falls (George H. Stanton, president) and the First State
Bank of Shelby (James A. Johnson, president) closed their doors.
Both denied that involvement of their executives in the fight promotion had any connection to the voluntary closings. The banks
insisted that neither Stanton nor Johnson used any funds from
their respective institutions in the financing of the fight.

Economic conditions in Montana had been deteriorating for
years, with other financial institutions closing and depositors losing confidence. In Shelby, where the citizens expressed certainty
that the local bank would reopen, a "slow run" did occur as the
fight's dire financial straits dominated the news.

The cashier L. A. Murrils said on July 10 that "many depositors drew out their money in the last two weeks, believing that funds of the bank might have been used by Mayor Johnson in connection with the Dempsey-Gibbons fight." On the afternoon of July 9, the First State Bank requested money to continue operating from its correspondent, Stanton Trust and Savings. Already in the process of liquidation, Stanton could not provide the necessary funds, forcing Johnson's bank to close.

On July 11 another Stanton Trust and Savings affiliate, the First State Bank of Joplin, locked its vault. "Newspaper reports from Joplin stated that all closings to date were 'generally accredited' to the championship boxing bout in Shelby."

For years afterward, people would say to Kearns, "You and Dempsey broke three banks with one fight." He considered that a misinformed slur. "We broke four," Kearns would respond, correcting the record.

The First National Bank of Shelby closed on August 16, "following withdrawals of something like a hundred thousand dollars in the first month after the fight," John Lardner wrote. "This left Shelby with, for the time being, no banks at all and practically no assets."

Whether those closings could, in fact, be attributed to actual financial losses from the fight, there must have been a related depletion of confidence among depositors at the very least. They probably ran no real risk of losing their savings, but, with two prominent bank presidents in deep, their concern seemed justified. It could not have helped the credibility of the bankers to have each soothing proclamation that everything would be fine proved wrong during the fight promotion. Combine that with the economic strain already strangling Montana in the early 1920s, and the people with accounts in those banks had sufficient reason to fear for their money.

In boxing circles and beyond, Shelby had become a national joke, not the sort of publicity Body Johnson had in mind. Every-

body had heard of the town by now, but they associated it with
the naive failure of its leaders. Anonymity must have seemed
preferable to that sort of embarrassing notoriety.

There was some sympathy for Shelby. Will Rogers, of all people,
could not find any humor in its misfortune:

*I have heard lots of kidding about Shelby's failure to raise so much money.
I generally try to see the funny side of our national calamities, including
politics, but to save my soul I can't think of a funny thing about Shelby,
Mont. They went into what they thought was a sporting proposition,
but they soon found out that about the only thing that was not connected
with it was sport.*

*They wanted to do something to put their little town on the map. They
believed in it; they believed, contrary to New York and all the so-called
experts, that Gibbons would make a creditable showing. They went out and
spent their money as far as it went, and that's as far as anyone can go.*

*Years ago, I remember a similar incident of a never-heard-of hustling
little town that was hardly known as far as the county line. . . . They,
like Shelby, wanted to do something that would attract attention to their
little town. . . . Now, if you are anxious to know what ever became of this
tank town, it's Tulsa, Okla., which would have been a real town even if
its people weren't greasy rich with oil, for it is founded on the spirit of
its people. They plunged and won. Shelby had the same spirit and lost. I
can't become tickled at it, myself.*

Rogers painted an accurate portrait of the local temperament.
Shelby did not wallow in defeat. It never achieved the Tulsa status
it sought, but the oil business continued bubbling, and the hard
feelings about the fight faded from festering wound to a fond
footnote in its history.

Loy Molumby returned to his law practice in Great Falls, maintaining a prominent and respected place in the community. Although active in Republican Party politics, including serving as
a Montana delegate to the national convention that nominated

Herbert Hoover in 1928, he made only one run for public office. As a candidate for mayor of Great Falls in 1928, he "lost out in a hotly contested race by around 60 votes."

His predominant interest remained the cause of military veterans. Molumby brought many cases seeking compensation on behalf of disabled servicemen, always pro bono. He once rented a home for "some 15 to 20 stranded veterans who were waiting for adjudication of their claims. Meal tickets, also provided by Molumby, furnished them with food while they waited."

As a former military pilot himself and a crusader on behalf of his fellow veterans, he had an image as a determined, selfless fighter. His tenacious effort to bring the Shelby fight to fruition reflected that trait. "Perhaps Molumby never more distinctly displayed his fighting spirit than when he interested himself in activities, without which there would have been no 'big fight' at Shelby."

Molumby spent one late January day in 1939 arguing a case at Choteau, Montana. Afterward, he had dinner at his ranch near Bynum with his manager, John Sabados. At about 1:00 a.m., he summoned Sabados to his bedside, where he had been stricken by a heart attack.

Within minutes, Molumby died at age forty-six, leaving behind a wife, three sisters, and his father. Members of the Montana National Guard and Legionnaires from around the state formed "an escort of honor and a firing squad" to bid farewell to their brother in arms.

James A. Johnson died about two months before Molumby, on November 23, 1938, at age seventy-three. His ill-fated association with the Dempsey-Gibbons fight appeared in the first sentence of his obituary, a prominent place in an eventful list of his life's work.

Though Johnson lost more than anyone on the fight's promotional failure, his diverse financial interests allowed him to recover over time. Leases on land in the oil fields north of Shelby, along with ranching and livestock concerns, helped restore his considerable portfolio.

"He never did, however, recover his old zip," Body Johnson said, "and, although we did not recognize it at the time, the fight did take a lot out of him physically, which I regret very much."

Johnson remained active in public life, in Shelby and beyond, serving as president of the Northwest Reclamation League. Its mission was to expand and enhance irrigation to six arid western states, and his work in that regard earned him mention as a potential U.S. secretary of the interior. Instead, he lived out his days in Shelby, which never became the next Tulsa but owed much of its growth to its first civic executive and most prominent citizen.

As a young businessman in 1923, Body Johnson had much less to lose than his father, despite the ill-fated idea of the fight originating with him. He must have been as surprised as anyone that it ever happened and certainly felt the most personal and professional remorse that his publicity scheme took on a life of its own. Time and the experiences of a long, active, and happy life did not change his mind or lull him into romanticizing the episode.

In 1925 he married Marjorie, the "same gal I took to the fight, but it took me two years to live it down before she said yes." Body and Marjorie had two children and seven grandchildren. After more than two decades as a businessman in Shelby, Johnson and his family moved to Spokane, Washington, in 1944, where he became a millionaire in his own right as "president and principal owner of three lumber companies and an oil company."

He pursued many recreational diversions, becoming a competent and competitive golfer, a 14-handicapper who won the Spokane club championship in his flight, as well as a hunter and fisherman. Reminiscing about the fight never appealed to him. Whenever Johnson happened to be in the same town as Jack

Dempsey or passed by the champion's restaurant in New York, he did not feel the gravitational pull of nostalgia. "I've always wanted to forget the whole thing," Johnson said.

Even into his nineties, the once sickly baby remained robust and disinclined to mine the history of the Shelby fiasco for fond memories. "No, I'm not glad that I did it. I'm not proud of it," Johnson said. "I was glad never to have anything to do with the fight business after that."

Tommy Gibbons had half a dozen more fights before retiring from the ring in 1925. He won four, with a no-decision against Georges Carpentier and a loss to Gene Tunney that ended his boxing career. Tunney went on to defeat Dempsey for the heavyweight title in 1926 and again in 1927.

Like his brother, Gibbons never won a world title, but he earned money and respect in the attempt while maintaining enough perspective to have a little fun at his own expense. His best source of income related to the Shelby fight came from the vaudeville contract he received as a result. "Though it didn't amount to much, it did help me a little," Gibbons said. "I had to compete with trained seals to get enough money to feed the wife and kids."

Unlike so many former boxers, Gibbons never became that kind of sideshow curiosity, and he never really struggled to pay the bills. Life outside the ring agreed with him, and he approached it with the same sober workaday dedication. In the first phase of his life after retiring from boxing, he became just another businessman in a suit and tie trying to make a living. He sold insurance, although he had access to potential clients that new salesmen did not. "I tried to sell Dempsey a $100,000 annuity," Gibbons said, "but at that time he and his manager, Jack Kearns, were being pushed around by a lot of people wanting money, and he turned it down."

Between his boxing and insurance income, Gibbons earned enough money by 1929 to subsidize the construction of Immaculate Conception Church in Osakis, Minnesota, where he had a lake home. "I was lucky to be able to build a church in Osakis when they needed one badly," Gibbons said. "It was an example to the kids to show them that spiritual values are the most important thing in life."

After almost a decade in the insurance business, Gibbons ran for sheriff of Ramsey County, Minnesota, home to St. Paul, where gambling, bootlegging, and worse were rampant. When he was elected in 1934, "there were slot machines and a few killings, and the bootleggers were turning to kidnapping," Gibbons said.

An FBI memo issued that year referred to St. Paul as "a haven for criminals. The citizenry knew it, the hoodlums knew it, and every police officer knew it." One of those hoodlums, the kidnapper Alvin "Creepy" Karpis, said that any criminal who had disappeared from his usual haunts for a while was either in prison or in St. Paul.

Compliant law enforcement helped embolden the criminal element in town until an FBI crackdown, including several high-profile trials, helped rid St. Paul of its roguish reputation. As the sheriff at the time, Gibbons received credit, which, along with his reputation for decency and fairness, helped his popularity flourish. He served twenty-four years, six terms, often running with little or no opposition at the polls. "Don't make a mistake," Gibbons said while reminiscing on the eve of his retirement in 1959. "The cleanup wasn't my doing. But I was in office when the FBI cleaned up the city."

Gibbons made it one of his top "clean-up" priorities to prevent as many messes as possible before they happened, focusing his preventative efforts on parents and children. His "junior sheriffs program" established a safety patrol system in the county schools, and he advised young people on the virtues of the straight and narrow. "Be fingerprint-shy. It's hard enough to get a good job without trouble in your past."

To parents, fathers in particular, he repeated a mantra about the importance of time spent together: "It's better to hunt with your kids than hunt for them." An avid outdoorsman and a devoted father of nine, Gibbons lived that slogan.

He and his first wife, Helen, had nine children. She died in 1939, and Gibbons remarried a year later. "I was lucky to get someone to move in on my nine youngsters," he said. Josephine also had three children of her own from a previous marriage.

Two of his nine children died in young adulthood. Jack Gibbons, the second oldest, who was almost four years old at the time of the Shelby fight, enrolled at the University of Notre Dame in the late 1930s. During the summer of 1941, he worked at Glacier National Park not far from Shelby, where he contracted an infection in his foot that killed him at age twenty-one.

On December 19, 1947, Mark Gibbons died of a heart condition after playing hockey with friends at St. John's University in Collegeville, Minnesota. The family's fifth child, Mark was twenty-three and engaged to be married.

As sheriff and, in a sense, a father figure to many area children other than his own, Gibbons carried on in the office he held with such esteem. Whenever children asked him for an autograph, he gave it in exchange for their signature on a "good citizenship" pledge, enrolling them in his "Good Government Club." For those kids he could not reach before they got into trouble, he made daily visits to the juveniles held in the Ramsey County jail to help steer them back toward a productive path.

His Shelby experience remained a warm memory—Gibbons was perhaps the only principal participant who felt that way—and a source of material for the banquet circuit. In 1958 he returned for the thirty-fifth anniversary of the fight, hailed as if he had not only competed against Dempsey but also defeated him. The elder "Thunder Chief," now with more weight and less hair, remained the popular choice of Shelby citizens. "I always get a kick out of those people," Gibbons said. "To them, I won the heavyweight championship."

On November 19, 1960, less than two years after his retirement, the sixty-nine-year-old Gibbons died in his sleep of an apparent heart attack. He appeared to be feeling well the night before, staying up late to answer correspondence. His wife, Josephine, found him dead the next morning. She said: "I don't think he struggled a bit."

Within months after the Shelby fight, the uneasy relationship between Dempsey and Kearns began to fray. It came apart at the seams by the spring of 1924 with, in essence, Dempsey cast in the role of Shelby and Kearns playing himself. The manager wanted all the money he could wring from the champion, and Dempsey began to bristle at his tactics and sense of entitlement. "Kearns freely spent his earnings," the writer Randy Roberts said, "and, whenever possible, he just as freely spent a portion of Dempsey's money." Still, it took a woman to drive the final wedge between them.

Dempsey fell in love with the actress Estelle Taylor and intended to marry her. As a matter of policy, Kearns did not believe that a fighter in the prime of his career should settle down, and he took a drunken train trip from New York to Los Angeles to remind Dempsey. To Kearns, a fighter had precious few years to be a major gate attraction. Avoiding the constraints of "home ties" helped maximize that earning potential. Or, as the writer Roger Kahn put it: "Kearns would put up with anything in a fighter except maturity."

Kearns made an ugly scene at the Montmartre Club in Los Angeles, threatening to divulge embarrassing information about Estelle he received from a private eye. She complained later that Dempsey did not defend her honor against that drunken bum, but he admitted a grudging respect for the man who helped make him. With more shrewdness than shame, she encouraged Dempsey's increasing instinct to break with Kearns.

For all their years together, Kearns and Dempsey had only an informal typewritten agreement that called for a fifty-fifty split of proceeds. Most state boxing commissions did not allow a manager to receive more than a third of his boxer's income, and Kearns originally forged Dempsey's signature on the document. (He later convinced Dempsey to trace over it so he could say that he "signed" it.)

Estelle looked over the agreement and could not deny the fifty-fifty split, but she also noticed it expired in August 1926. Wait until September of that year to fight again, she said, and Kearns would have no claim on Dempsey's share of the purse. He did exactly that, participating only in European exhibitions until facing Gene Tunney on September 23, 1926, in his first title defense in three years. (Dempsey defeated Luis Angel Firpo in New York two months after winning in Shelby.)

Long before that Tunney fight, even before Dempsey formed his legal partnership with Estelle on February 7, 1925, his relationship with Kearns had dissolved, though the paperwork bound them together for another eighteen months. To the public, their partnership was like a marriage, and the troubled state of it became a source of great curiosity. After the wedding ceremony a reporter asked, "Champ, did you invite Doc Kearns?"

"I didn't ask him because I knew he wouldn't come," Dempsey said.

That more or less confirmed the rumors of their split, but the partnership was already not exclusive. With Dempsey's blessing, Kearns became the welterweight champion Mickey Walker's manager. Walker lost that title in 1926 but soon defeated Tiger Flowers for the middleweight championship.

In his first attempt for the middleweight crown, Walker lost a fifteen-round decision to Harry Greb. According to legend, Walker and Greb took their ongoing debate about the outcome from a saloon into the New York streets later that same night. If a middleweight champ did not attract the heavyweight box office receipts Kearns preferred, Walker at least shared Kearns's spirit for both fighting and living hard. They seemed to be a better match in that regard. "Around Kearns," Walker said, "every night was New Year's Eve."

At first, in the chaos of establishing himself as his own manager, Dempsey tended to romanticize his years with Kearns. "Keep away from that lousy bastard, Jack," Estelle said, and he did, but Kearns would not leave him alone. "A resourceful ally, Kearns was just as crafty as an enemy," Roberts said, "and from the time he split with Dempsey, he was the champion's foremost adversary."

Three lawsuits filed for a combined total of more than $700,000 kept Kearns in the front of the champion's mind. One of the suits sought damages of $333,333.33, the amount Kearns alleged to be due him for a Dempsey-Wills fight that never happened. All three eventually were thrown out, but it took years, and Kearns used whatever strong-arm tactics he could to provoke Dempsey. During the champ's training in upstate New York for the 1926 Tunney fight, Estelle was driving near Saratoga in a Rolls Royce when police stopped her. A man named Abner Siegel, claiming to be a lawyer for Kearns, accompanied the cop and insisted he would be attaching the car as part of the former manager's legal claim.

The car was impounded despite Estelle producing the registration in her name, and the men escorted her back to Dempsey's camp. Siegel climbed a fence to serve papers on the champion in training. Stress from this harassment took a noticeable physical toll on Dempsey. Recurring boils pocked his skin, and he drank a glass of olive oil every morning to combat constipation. Writers covering his training camp thought he looked sick. Whether it was age, rust, or the upsetting intrusions of Kearns, he had lost something—weight, legs, power behind his punches, something.

At the fight, Kearns watched from ringside with Mark Kelly, a reporter from Los Angeles. He sensed the title slipping away but saw ways Dempsey could overcome the effects of time and personal turmoil to defeat Tunney.

"Get over to his corner and help him," Kelly said, but pride trumped the instinct to help.

"No. Let him take it," Kearns said. "That's the way he wanted it and that's the way it will have to be."

As he listened, Kelly noticed Kearns was crying, but he offered a halfhearted denial about humidity or some other cause of the precipitation in his eyes.

"You're not kidding me. You're crying, you bum," Kelly said. "Go on. Get up in the corner and help him."

Kearns refused, but he felt the remorse of the moment. "No matter what comes between two people," he said, "if you have fought hard times together and made good it doesn't all disappear."

That night in Philadelphia, for Dempsey and Kearns alike, it all disappeared. Perhaps for Kearns, the tears flowed because he missed out on a share of a $1.9 million gate. Dempsey cried through bruised and swollen eyes, not because he lost, but because the crowd cheered the fallen champion in defeat like he had never heard before.

A man who symbolized the Roaring Twenties, Dempsey saw his championship career end well before the end of the decade. Like so many others, he lost most of his earnings in the 1929 stock market crash. His celebrity allowed him a variety of options, however demeaning they might have seemed to a former heavyweight champion of the world. Dempsey fought exhibitions and even officiated at wrestling matches, rebuilding his wealth in dire economic conditions. In 1935, he opened a restaurant that, like Dempsey himself, would become a New York institution.

During World War II, Dempsey served in the U.S. Coast Guard. Though he was far too old to enlist, his application benefited from "some high-level intervention, perhaps by Franklin D. Roosevelt." He spent most of his time overseeing physical training at a base in Brooklyn, but he accompanied a unit onto the island of Okinawa on April 1, 1945. The forty-nine-year-old former champion received praise in equal proportion to the criticism he endured over his role in World War I. Neither felt right to him. "You know," he told the writer Roger Kahn, "in World War I they said I was a slacker. In World War II they said I was a hero. They were wrong both times."

For most of his long life outside the ring, Dempsey would be revered as a sports hero, the living legend of a golden era. He greeted visitors to his restaurant from his corner booth with a graciousness that became his defining characteristic.

After a series of strokes in the late 1970s, heart trouble compounded his health problems, and Dempsey died on May 31, 1983, an eighty-seven-year-old man still remembered as the rugged slugger of the 1920s.

Kearns never managed another fighter with Dempsey's talent and star power, but he never sacrificed his flair to the fluctuating athletic and economic fortunes either. In a 1953 *Esquire* profile the "fastest man in a fast racket" leaped off the page in living color, wearing those curious hues—burnt orange blazer, dark blue shirt, yellow tie—that matched his colorful personality, if not the other pieces in his ensemble. "On him, they look right." Thirty years after Shelby, busy rebuilding the fortune he made and spent many times over, Kearns did not pause for reflection or make any apology. If anything, he said, the ingrates in Shelby should be glad he never sued them for the money they still owed him. To Kearns, what happened there just reflected his most basic operating philosophy. "I was always looking out for my fighter," he said. "What happened to them other fellas was their lookout."

Kearns lived another forty years and three days after slipping out of Shelby, his last waking moments spent thinking about a trip to Las Vegas for the second Liston-Patterson fight scheduled for July 22, 1963. He died on July 7 at age eighty with, as his son put it, the mind of a 21-year-old and the body of a 125-year old.

The *Los Angeles Times* columnist Jim Murray eulogized him in ink as the last of his kind. Probably the first too, or at least the best at boxing's true objective: to accumulate money from the willing or the naive and spend it among the purveyors of life's indulgences.

Murray pulled no punches, figuring "there must be a no-limit crap game going on in the Great Beyond today. Or a high-stake poker game with a marked deck. Or some kind of grift. Otherwise, Doc Kearns never would have left here. Maybe there's a nice little town that should be bilked. Or a nice little guy whose pockets are leaking money and he trusts people. Maybe some fight manager has been careless enough to leave his boy's contract lying around unsigned."

Heaped on someone without Doc's unvarnished charm and willingness to buy the next round (and the next and the next), those might have sounded like accusations. From Murray's inspired pen, it read like affection for a man whose death marked the extinction of a species of a particular, peculiar array of colors.

"The eyewitness stuff Doc took with him when he went to sleep in Miami the other night is more precious than a mountain of warmed-over clippings, the raw ore of a life and gaudy times we shall never see again of a vanishing breed of American who was still hustling around at the age of 81 [sic] and searching his few remaining locks for one last fingernail of gold dust."

The legend did not die with Kearns. A couple of fight fans sitting around the Tropicana in Las Vegas pondered where he would spend eternity—fistic philosophy over coffee. One of them said Doc undoubtedly would go to heaven, whether he deserved it or not, because he always traveled first-class even if he had only a beer budget to spend on his champagne habits. Sure, the other guy said, and if St. Peter pulled the book on him, not only would Doc con the pearly gate keeper into letting him into heaven; he'd get a percentage of the gate.

Bibliography

A feature by Robert K. Elder in the *Chicago Tribune* brought the Dempsey-
Gibbons saga to my attention and inspired the idea to write a book about it.
For a while it remained just that—an idea. When I learned that the University
of Notre Dame, about five minutes from my house, held an extensive boxing
archive, it began to gather momentum.

I e-mailed George Rugg, a curator in the Department of Special Collections
at the Hesburgh Libraries of Notre Dame, with a long-winded description
of the event. It was news to me, so I provided as much detail as I could to
help him unearth anything that might be in his files.

His quick response might as well have included an eye-rolling emoti-
con. It said something to the effect of, "Yeah, we've got that." In its time,
Dempsey-Gibbons was a big deal, not only as a heavyweight title fight but
also as an irresistible tale of Shelby's small-town ambition and the big-time
greed that ambushed it. The fascinating material that Rugg curates, including
a wealth of clippings from the files of *Ring* magazine in the Stanley Weston
Collection, helped provide the foundation to tell that tale.

Issues of the *Boxing Blade* from 1923 were especially helpful. Mike Collins
became embroiled in the Shelby affair by accident, but, as the editor of the

Blade, he had rare access for a journalist through his role as "matchmaker." Over several issues in July and August 1923, he reported his experiences in Shelby, the closest a researcher could get to interviewing a principal (and relatively objective) figure in the promotion.

James "Body" Johnson provided a similar service to posterity many years later with his own account, published first in *Sports Illustrated* and later as a book called *The Fight That Won't Stay Dead* (Shelby MT: Promoter, 1989). Johnson argued that the lying of Jack Kearns doomed the fight to financial failure, but his own deception triggered the whole escapade in the first place, which he also acknowledged in his rueful manifesto.

Kearns admitted (and lived up to) his own reputation for "gilding the lily" in his autobiography *The Million Dollar Gate* (New York: Macmillan, 1966), which included his side of the Shelby affair.

Many writers who were there, and plenty who were not, seemed to romanticize the fantastic events of the spring and summer of 1923. Bill Corum, a young reporter for the *New York Times* in those days, was one of the first journalists to arrive in Shelby. Both his reporting and the reminiscing in his memoir *Off and Running* (New York: Holt, 1959) were integral to reconstructing the story.

Dozens of other sources, including Dempsey biographies, newspaper and magazine articles, and the Montana PBS documentary *Ringside Shelby* (2003), to name just a few, contributed important insights and information.

I tried to keep my judgments to a minimum, to let the facts, as far as they could be verified, speak for themselves. In cases where some sifting of conflicting information was required—like the matter of how and when Dempsey's contract came to be worth $300,000—I attempted to present all sides and explain clearly how I reached a conclusion. Any mistakes or misjudgments are my own.

For interested readers and researchers, notes on sources for each chapter follow.

1. High Noon in Shelby

Most of the color and detail of July 4, 1923, in Shelby came from the reporting of the *Great Falls Tribune*, the *New York Times*, and the Associated Press, all of which covered the fight with, well, great color and detail.

Charles Samuels, in a January 1953 profile of Kearns in *True Magazine*, described the "dynamite in the air" atmosphere inside the arena before the fight. Bill Corum remembered the actual exploding firecracker that caused an instant of fear about gunfire in his *Off and Running*.

All the mind reading of Tommy Gibbons in his corner came from his own account (available at the University of Notre Dame archive), *How I Fought the Champs* (as told to Les Etter), which described his mentality before the fight and his plan to defeat Dempsey. He described the scene from his perspective, down to the sound of Dempsey's high-pitched voice when the fighters met at the center of the ring.

2. Boom and Bust

Peter Shelby's quote that the town named for him "will never amount to a damn" appears in several places, including *The Hi-Line: Profiles of a Montana Land* (Helena MT: American & World Geographic Publishing, 1993) by Daniel N. Vichorek. The description that Great Northern Railroad officials "threw a boxcar from the train and called it a station" also pops up in multiple historical accounts of Shelby.

"Feast or Famine" by B. Derek Strahn in the Spring 2007 issue of *Distinctly Montana* was helpful in providing a history of homesteading and the boom-bust pattern in the state.

Information on oil discovery in the region, and its impact on Shelby, came from *Great Falls Tribune* coverage of the biggest business news in the region.

James A. Johnson's personal history appeared in Body Johnson's *The Fight That Won't Stay Dead* and the former mayor's obituary in the *Great Falls Tribune*. Body Johnson also outlined his frail arrival in the world, the family's leading role in Shelby's business and politics, and how the local American Legion got into the boxing business to help entertain the oil men.

The *Great Falls Tribune* covered the boxing club's first successful fight promotion on January 26, 1923. It made what turned out to be an ominous statement that "the attendance seems to justify the securing of better talent and staging another series of bouts in the near future."

Body Johnson's account described the fateful moment when he and Mel McCutcheon came up with their publicity stunt and how they decided to pursue Gibbons as an opponent for Dempsey.

3. The Cerebral Slugger

The story of Mike Gibbons making his professional debut in an illegal fight that the chief of police promoted came from an online tribute to Minneapolis and St. Paul boxers: http://www.tmgps.com/Mike%20Gibbons%20Biography%20By%20George%20Blair.htm.

Harry Greb's comment to his manager after fighting Mike Gibbons—"From now on, match me with one guy at a time"—appears in many places, including *The Boxing Register* (Ithaca NY: McBooks, 1999).

Information about Minnesota boxing history came from stories in the *St. Paul Pioneer Press* and the *Minneapolis Tribune* in the files and microfilm collection at the public library in downtown Minneapolis.

A 1952 story by *Minneapolis Tribune* writer George Barton described Mike Gibbons's arrest and the fine that exceeded his purse from a 1908 fight. It was also the *Minneapolis Tribune* coverage of the Tommy Gibbons–Billy Miske fight from July 13 and 14, 1915, that provided information about that bout and associated finances.

Information about Gibbons increasing his stature in the fight game and his quote that he has "longed for . . . the heavyweight classic" came from clippings in the Stanley Weston Collection at Notre Dame.

The *New York Times* on March 14, 1922, provided the information about the Gibbons-Greb fight at Madison Square Garden.

Details about Gibbons's fluctuating reputation after his loss to Greb, including his brother's criticism, came from the Weston Collection at Notre Dame.

Coverage of Gibbons's fight against Billy Miske, including the impending news of his father's death, came from the *New York Times* and the *Boxing Blade*. Both publications also included commentary suggesting that Gibbons deserved to win and that he did not foul Miske as the referee determined.

The *Times* also provided the details from the Gibbons-Miske rematch two months later that helped reestablish Gibbons's status as a top contender for Dempsey's title.

4. A Shark Takes the Bait

The *Great Falls Tribune* reported the boxing news of early 1923, the typical bickering of managers and promoters, without any indication of a potential local connection—until its February 8, 1923, editions published the telegrams Lyman Sampson sent to Kearns and Collins.

Throughout the coming days, weeks, and months, the Great Falls newspaper continued to report the ongoing developments in the negotiations. Much of the detail about those events also came from Collins's own recollections in the *Boxing Blade* in the late summer of 1923. Body Johnson also provided insight and information about that time frame in *The Fight That Won't Stay Dead*.

Johnson reprinted the letter from Loy J. Molumby describing his personal opinion about Dempsey and how he hoped the champion would lose his title in Montana.

Collins recounted his first encounter with Shelby and all its enthusiastic citizens in the *Boxing Blade*, and *Great Falls Tribune* coverage of the same events confirmed much of his description.

5. Sticky Fingers

Most of the travel log about the earthy early life of Jack Kearns came from his autobiography *The Million Dollar Gate*, which benefits and suffers from his own tendency to exaggerate. It is hard to trust him, but it is impossible not to want to believe the yarns he spins.

Benjamin Estelle Lloyd published the pungent description of the Barbary Coast—"the haunt of the low and the vile of every kind"—in *Lights and Shades of San Francisco* (San Francisco: Bancroft, 1876). That was perhaps the only part of the chapter Kearns could not have said better himself.

Roger Kahn's *A Flame of Pure Fire: Jack Dempsey and the Roaring '20s* (New York: Harcourt Brace, 1999) detailed the 1919 title fight against Jess Willard. It also described Willard's fatal blow against John "Bull" Young and the champion's fear that he might do the same to Dempsey. Kearns quoted himself in *The Million Dollar Gate* as telling reporters that Willard "couldn't kill a midget if they gave him an axe."

The quote that Kearns "unlimbered the golden touch that he had been developing since he was fourteen" was Jack O'Brien's from a July 1953 *Esquire* profile, "The Spellbinder." O'Brien also painted the colorful picture of Kearns's wardrobe, down to the cane heaved out of a bar after him one night in London. Charles Samuels's profile in *True* added more hues to the vibrant Kearns rainbow.

6. A $300,000 IOU

The recollection of the Sioux-Blackfoot battle on the site of the proposed Shelby arena appeared in the *Great Falls Tribune* on March 24, 1923, along with the comparison to the Roman Coliseum.

Collins fanned the excitement in the region with his comments in the *Great Falls Tribune* about the prospects for a successful promotion.

Body Johnson described how "hell was popping on the home front" as publicity exceeded his capacity to control. This was when he made the unfortunate decision to mislead the local American Legion Boxing Club, a key factor in the stunt turning into reality.

In his *Boxing Blade* series, Collins explained the twists and turns of the negotiations, including the manager Eddie Kane's suggestion that Gibbons could fight on a percentage basis. Back in Montana, the promoters were not deterred by Kearns's stalling tactics, pursuing him by train and plane. The *Great Falls Tribune* reports of their efforts were based on communications with Molumby. American Legion opposition to Dempsey's participation also appeared in that newspaper.

Toward the end of April, after weeks of exhaustive effort to reach a deal, the *Great Falls Tribune* reported a $300,000 offer for Dempsey, attributed to Kane. This was more than a week before the official signing, and it contradicted Body Johnson's claim that a $300,000 guarantee had not been mentioned before the contract became official. It appeared several times before the May 5 signing.

Johnson described the party at the Morrison Hotel in Chicago, where he believed a drunken Molumby signed the contract—"with the help of an awful lot of Champagne and whiskey"—during an interview in the documentary *Ringside Shelby*.

The complications that arose in making the first $100,000 payment to Kearns came from Collins in the *Boxing Blade*, though the *Great Falls Tribune* reported the brimming confidence of the promoters. More skepticism appeared in the *New York Times*, as boxing officials wondered how this unknown town could handle the finances and logistics of a heavyweight title fight.

7. The Circus Comes to Town

Mike Collins noted in the *Boxing Blade* that Shelby did not exactly get to work on all the necessary details with due dispatch. He outlined the difficulty the promoters encountered in attracting contractors for the arena and how the bidding process proceeded.

The *Great Falls Tribune* heralded Dempsey's arrival in town on May 15, painting a vivid scene of the warm welcome he received. Descriptions of Dempsey on that day, and later at the livestock auction, along with quotes attributed to him, came from the local paper's coverage.

Information about the interest he developed in his youth for animals and the outdoors came from Toby Smith's *Kid Blackie: Jack Dempsey's Colorado Days* (Ouray CO: Wayfinder, 1987).

Kearns described his own extracurricular activities, including the "corn-haired . . . Annie Oakley" he became well acquainted with, in *The Million Dollar Gate*.

The *Great Falls Tribune*, the *New York Times*, and other papers were provided daily dispatches from Shelby by mid-May 1923, describing the progress in ticket sales and construction. All the papers also provided the details from Dempsey's training camp, which opened while Gibbons remained on a state exhibition tour.

Kearns described his first visit to Shelby, including the "fly-infested luncheon" where he did his typical lily gilding, in *The Million Dollar Gate*. Eating it up, the *Great Falls Tribune* reported the manager's empty promises with hope that they might come true.

"What's the use of winding clocks" Shelby's mayor, James A. Johnson, wondered in the *Great Falls Tribune*, which also reported on the fleeting strike threats facing local contractors.

The paper also detailed the banquet at the end of Gibbons's exhibition tour and Dempsey's perilous vacation trip down the side of a cliff.

8. Checks and Balances

The *Minneapolis Tribune* covered the boisterous local send-off for Gibbons on June 6, 1923, including the good-luck charms he received. At the other end of the Great Northern line in Shelby, the *Great Falls Tribune* continued the story of civic excitement, "the greatest . . . the town has known since the railroad came."

News from Dempsey's training camp, inside the ring and out, also came from the *Great Falls Tribune*.

Gibbons discussed his visit to the University of Minnesota to study the science of boxing in the *New York Times*.

The *Minneapolis Journal* described the living arrangements of the Gibbons family and Gibbons's sparring partners on his arrival in Shelby.

Though the *Minneapolis Journal* made fun of them, the ongoing first-person print fisticuffs between Dempsey and Gibbons in the *Minneapolis Tribune* were a treat, regardless of who might have written them.

Soon enough, a throng of reporters arrived from around the country, adding to the information emanating from Shelby. They did some reporting on the "tough element" that also found its way into town. That prompted the state attorney general to insist on "moral conditions" in Shelby, as reported by the *Great Falls Tribune*.

The *Great Falls Tribune* also published notices of several arrests and disturbances, including the lovers' quarrel later described in more personal detail in Corum's memoir. Despite all that, the local sheriff insisted that the town would be clean, including the quote in the *Great Falls Tribune* about tossing gambling machines into the river. The paper sent an undercover reporter to survey the available vices, to no avail, concluding, "Shelby is a closed town."

Corum recalled the "hair-tinted and beauty-lotioned" Patricia Salmon and the visiting scribes who inflated her appeal.

In addition to training details from the Gibbons camp, the *New York Times* reported on the challenger's afternoon gopher hunt. Body Johnson's book and Collins's series of stories each reported that Kearns promised in private that the fight would go on regardless of payment in full. If the promoters had their way, they would have waited until Dempsey climbed in the ring before he got a dime. Johnson quoted Jim Speer as saying, "I don't trust this bastard and I advise you to keep the money until the day of the fight." He also described the "threat" Kearns received from the old football all-American named Kelly and said that the promoters "just couldn't believe that anyone could be the liar that Kearns turned out to be."

Information on the plane crash came from Johnson's book and the *Great Falls Tribune*. That jarring event complicated the office atmosphere, which "could be described as a hypothyroid mess," Johnson said in *The Fight That Won't Stay Dead*.

"One-Eyed" Connolly's arrival merited a mention in the *Great Falls Tribune*, which continued to provide updates on training and the myriad issues surrounding the fight. The *New York Times* first noted the "pessimism" about the availability of the second installment to Kearns. In *The Million Dollar Gate*, Kearns described the offer of livestock in lieu of that payment and his refusal of an offer to take over the promotion himself. Dan Tracy did take over the promotion, and his lengthy statement as he assumed control appeared in the *New York Times*.

As attention returned to the ring, the *Minneapolis Tribune* reported Rocco Stramalgia's comment comparing Dempsey and Gibbons from his sparring experience.

Body Johnson's quote that Kearns "would lie like hell and he did it time after time" came from the documentary *Ringside Shelby*.

9. Under Water

Kearns refuted persistent claims that Dempsey was out of shape in the *Great Falls Tribune*.

Details of Gibbons the family man, at peace cradling his infant son, appeared in a King Feature Service article by Frank G. Menke.

Kane's comment that he and Gibbons would "let Dempsey get the money, we'll take the title" was published in the *New York Times*.

The staring contest Gibbons hoped to win as a psychological advantage, and Dempsey's interest in pinochle, came from their respective first-person pieces in the *Minneapolis Tribune*.

The writer Robert Edgren, in Shelby covering the fight, reported Kearns's frequent wardrobe changes and the manager's quote that "the only new proposition I can hear has to have a rustle like $100,000."

Several papers reported the hoax of a telegram promising to pay the final $100,000 installment.

The *Great Falls Tribune* covered the ceremony where Gibbons became "Thunder Chief," a member of the Blackfoot tribe.

James A. Johnson's bold declaration, "You can tell the cock-eyed world that the battle will come off . . . with bells on," appeared in the *Great Falls Tribune*.

Kearns remembered the tent shows in town, not to mention Aunt Kate's Cathouse, in *The Million Dollar Gate*.

Most of the detail about the all-day negotiations on July 2 came from the *New York Times* and the *Great Falls Tribune*.

Frank Walker made a cameo appearance in *The Million Dollar Gate* and recounted his participation in notes for his own memoir. Walker, a future postmaster general of the United States and a young lawyer from Butte in 1923, was summoned to help the promoters handle Kearns. The Frank C. Walker Papers at the University of Notre Dame, where he graduated from law school, offered his side of his brief but memorable role in the Shelby affair. Corum's memoir also mentioned Walker and, in fact, prompted the lawyer to set the record straight, although the differences in his and Corum's accounts were subtle.

Grantland Rice's memoir, *The Tumult and the Shouting: My Life in Sport* (New York: A. S. Barnes, 1954), included the quote about how the reporters "had long since gone nuts" trying to keep up with developments in Shelby.

Details of how those "Scribes Persuade Champ's Manager to Take a Chance" were reported by the Associated Press and published in numerous newspapers, including the *Minneapolis Journal*.

Kearns recounted his own mind-set—"we might as well collect from those who still hadn't bought tickets"—in *The Million Dollar Gate*.

Heywood Broun's amusing "prediction" about the fight, courtesy of the fortuneteller Esmerelda, came from the *Minneapolis Tribune*.

10. Standing Their Ground

Information about the fight itself, and the scene in and around the arena, came from numerous newspaper reports and the *Boxing Blade*. The quote attributed to a security officer—"If you don't have the guts to break in, then stay out"—was in the documentary *Ringside Shelby*.

Gibbons also contributed to the detail about the fight, specifically his own physical and mental state, in his recollection *How I Fought the Champs*.

John Lardner described Dempsey's "farewell" from Great Falls with a small group shouting, "Don't hurry back," in "The Sack of Shelby," published in the *New Yorker* and collected in *White Hopes and Other Tigers* (New York: J. B. Lippincott, 1951).

Kearns described his getaway from Shelby and the night in the basement of a Great Falls barbershop in *The Million Dollar Gate*.

Body Johnson's quote that Kearns "prevailed upon the revenue people to give him the money" was in *The Fight That Won't Stay Dead*. Rasmussen, the IRS agent, said otherwise in the *Great Falls Tribune*.

Jack Skees described the harrowing work of delivering the fight films to idling airplanes in *Ringside Shelby*.

The Associated Press reported James A. Johnson's wry request for "the price of a shave" after the fight.

11. A Cut of Heaven's Gate

Richard Henry Little of the *Chicago Tribune* painted a picture of Shelby returning to normalcy in the aftermath of the fight.

In *The Fight That Won't Stay Dead*, Body Johnson reprinted the final financial statement his father submitted to the American Legion Boxing Club.

The *Great Falls Tribune* estimated losses to concessionaires and the rodeo and stampede and reported the closing of the Stanton Bank in Great Falls and the First State Bank of Shelby, both within a week of the fight. Lardner detailed other bank closings attributed to the financial duress of the promotion in "The Sack of Shelby."

Will Rogers's lamentation about the laughter at Shelby's expense appeared in the *Great Falls Tribune*.

Information about Loy Molumby's life after Shelby came from a detailed obituary in the *Great Falls Tribune*. The newspaper also reported on James A. Johnson's death and, combined with Body Johnson's reminiscing about his father, provided the foundation for recounting his life's work.

Information about Body Johnson's life came from his book, a *Sports Illustrated* introduction to his story about Shelby, and the *Ringside Shelby* documentary, where he said, "I'm not proud of it. I was glad never to have anything to do with the fight business after that."

Gibbons remained a public figure as the sheriff of Ramsey County, Minnesota. Much of his life story came from interviews with Twin Cities newspapers and his first-person accounts of experiences in the ring. Additional family information came from the Tommy and Mike Gibbons Preservation Society, online at http://www.tmgps.com.

Two biographies, in particular, were invaluable in researching parts of Dempsey's well-chronicled life. Roger Kahn's *A Flame of Pure Fire* and Randy Roberts's *Jack Dempsey: The Manassa Mauler* (Baton Rouge: Louisiana State University Press, 1979) detailed his rocky relationship with Kearns and the women in his life, among other important information.

Kearns explained the emotions felt as he watched Dempsey lose the title in *The Million Dollar Gate*.

Newspaper and magazine articles about Jack Kearns, including Jim Murray's obituary and the story of the men sitting around the Tropicana coffee shop discussing his fate in the afterlife, came from clippings in the Stanley Weston Collection at Notre Dame.